From Broken to Blessed

A True Story of Redemption

From Broken to Blessed

A True Story of Redemption

Brenda Tiller Martin

East Hartford, Connecticut 06108

From Broken to Blessed

ISBN 978-0-692-91070-2

Cover Design: Donna Osborn Clark at CreationsByDonna@gmail.com

Layout and Interior Design: www.CreationByDonna.com

Editing: Timothy G. Green at Inkaissance: inkaissance@gmail.com

Typing and Proof Reading: Kelly O'Brien at kellyobrien2892@gmail.com

Published by: JIJ Productions

East Hartford, Connecticut 06108

Scriptures from the following versions of the *Holy Bible*:

Holy Bible, New Living Translation, copyright © 1996, 2004, 2015 by Tyndale House Foundation. Used by permission of Tyndale House Publishers Inc., Carol Stream, Illinois 60188. All rights reserved.

Holy Bible, New Life Version © Christian Literature International

First Edition

I dedicate this book to God, who is the head of my life.

Acknowledgments

I would like to give honor to God for giving me a second chance at life, for taking my mess and turning it into my message. A special thanks to my coworker Kelly O'Brien for all the time she spent with me helping to recall events of my life, for typing, editing, and helping me to make this book possible. I will forever be grateful. I would to thank my parents JD and Irene Tiller for loving me unconditionally and being there for me. My brother Johnny Tiller. I want to thank my son Keith Anthony Martin Jr. for loving me and not turning his back on me when I needed him the most. I know it was hard to grow up with a mother on crack cocaine, but he always acknowledged me as his mother. My grandson Anthony Dennis Martin, my granddaughter Laila Dior Martin who always says, "I've got my eyes on you, Grandma." My uncle John D. Tiller. A special thanks to my Apostle Eugene Taylor for all the prayers over the years and for listening to God's voice and allowing me to praise God. It was through my praise that I received my deliverance. Also for every phone call he answered and for his wife Robin Taylor. Deacon Maxine Dean. A special thanks to Apostle Kathy Hughes for prophesying over my life because she saw the good in me when I was in the middle of my mess. All my church members at Agape Fellowship Ministry. Coretha Thomas. All my friends. A special thanks to Karen Scott for helping me with every dream that I have had to come true. From graduating school and being there to help me when I couldn't even write a sentence. A special thanks to Noel Scott for sharing his wife with me over the years. And the rest of the Washington family Donna, Vickie, and Elliot. A special thanks to Gloria White. My cousins Betty and Robert Brown, my Aunt and Uncle Jim and Christine Thomas. All my coworkers at CMHA and all my coworkers at HARC. A special thanks to Margaret Medlin, and a special thanks to Tora Medlin for the photo shoot. A special thanks to Donna Osborn Clark for being patient with me and walking me through every process of the book and making my dream come true, and Timothy Green for doing an excellent job with editing.

Introduction

This book is a testimony of the strength and faithfulness of God being with you even when you aren't aware of His presence. All of us go through joys and pains and we each have a story. I believe that my story may not be so different from yours. Even though there are similarities, my story is mine. It is the one thing that cannot be taken away from me. As you read this testimony I hope that you praise my God with me for His grace and mercy that allowed me to make it. If you are being oppressed in any way, let this testimony stir your spirit to know that you too can be set free.

I have been set free; from broken to blessed.

Psalm 121:1New Life Version (NLV)

The Lord—Our Helper

[121] I will lift up my eyes to the mountains. Where will my help come from?

Chapter 1

MY SOUTHERN CHILDHOOD DELIGHTS

I was born in the South, raised in a small town called Newville, Alabama. We lived on a farm in those days. I can remember picking cotton and doing it so well that my parents made me my own gathering bag. It had the kind of shoulder strap that could fit around my neck which allowed me to drag it. However, that all changed when the weight was overbearing and demanded that I dumped it. This was the foundation building of my strong work ethic that I am blessed to still have today.

My brother Johnny, who I called June, was a year older than me. He never wanted to pick cotton. Instead, he spent the majority of his time catching bugs. That was his true delight. It didn't seem to matter what kind of bugs he caught as long as he was catching bugs. However, he soon learned that there were consequences while chasing bugs on the job. Every Saturday when it came time for the workers to be paid he could not stand in line with us. This made him so angry it was frightful. Nonetheless, the bug chasing still continued.

After every payday our parents would take us into town to get groceries and household supplies. After laboring so hard at work this became the biggest day of our week. The town's general store not only sold food and other provisions but it also sold toys. It was so nice to get a new doll or something for my playhouse. This became an early teaching for the importance of self care.

A highlight of my childhood was playing with my dolls in the backyard or in my playhouse. I discovered a great idea on how to light a fire in my playhouse. I put two bricks together that served as a stove on which I cooked fresh eggs over an open fire. It was pretty ingenious for such a little girl. Of course, I always wanted someone to come out to my house and eat with me. Mom was a good candidate, but she would refuse me every time. However, dad would always sample my cooking. He would constantly tell me what a great cook I was. This encouraged my childhood ego to cook as much as I could to impress my daddy. His affection was not only appreciated, but it was desperately needed too.

I often played alone. Once in a while some girls from up the street would come over and play, but most of the time I was alone. I was a girly girl who loved decorating my playhouse, dressing up and wearing my mother's jewelry. But most of all I *loved* to wear her three-inch heels! I felt beautiful in my mother's heels, while being eloquently dressed up and combing the hair of my babies. Oh yes, they were dolls. But, they were my babies. Their hair had to be perfected by my hands!

One Sunday after church a friend's mother asked my mother and I what poem I would be reciting for Easter service. I proudly and boldly recited it before them, as if I was before an audience. This would serve as one of my first childhood lessons on jealousy and covetousness. I will never forget that Sunday morning. I went to church totally prepared and anxious to show my efforts and preparation for that important day. I was so excited and could not wait to recite my poem before the church. This was going to be done for God's glory and in honor of my family. I practiced so hard to do my very best for both.

Just before I was called to speak they called my friend up instead. She was the daughter of the lady who had asked my mom what poem I was going to recite for the Easter service. To my surprise my friend got up and recited the exact same poem! I was so hurt, but I learned a valuable lesson that day. My mother refused to be discouraged and instead encouraged me to speak my poem in spite of. Even though I feared that the entire church would think that I stole her idea, I stood before the church and spoke those words from my heart. It was so passionate; as if it was the first time those words were ever spoken together. It doesn't matter what people try to take from you or whether they try to outshine you with malice. You only need to give what is from your heart and it will separate what is real from what is phony. I felt each word as though it was real. The church responded to the boldness that was released from deep inside my heart. I was a winner! Yes, I was a winner. Later on in life this lesson of overcoming simple adversity taught me how to be strong and bold. It would serve as a defense mechanism for when deeper and bigger things who confront me and try to take my breath away.

Memories flood me with how life was then compared to how life is now.

We waited inside of our house for the school bus. The driver would pull up outside and blow the horn to summon us to come out and get on board for the journey. Newville High School was the school we attended from 1st to 12th grade. It was an all black school and it was on one level. We had a homecoming at the last football game of the school year. It was called a "Little Miss" homecoming. They would crown one participant from the 1st grade and one from the 12th grade. The winner was determined by the person who raised the most money. I was in the first grade at the time.

My mom determined it would be me to raise the most money. She would come to school daily at noon and sell candied apples and bologna sandwiches. She was diligent and faithful in helping me. Her commitment was amazing and I admired it dearly. I remember being in my classroom and hearing the announcement of the winner ring loud and clear to the entire school. They called my name; MY name! Brenda Tiller!!! It rang so fully in my soul that it nearly startled me.

Mom was so proud of me and of course of her "considerable" accomplishments in the matter. She held me closer than ever; so close that I felt her heartbeat and her love from everything within her. Of course the occasion of winning demanded that I dress up in my best. I wore a pretty red velvet jumper with a can-can slip underneath it. I paired it with a pretty white blouse. Of course, white ruffled lace ankle socks were a must for the esteemed and honored *girl of the moment.* My shoes of choice were the traditional black patent leather shoes with black heels. My hair was in ponytails with red and white twists. A lady named Mrs. Cloise, whom my parents worked for on her farm, allowed me to wear her beautiful broach.

At the homecoming I had to wear a pretty blue glittered sash across my dress. I loved getting all dressed up and going before the school as the winner, until I was placed on the platform in front of everyone. I was stuck up there and could not play with the other children. I was devastated because this was one of the biggest school days of the year! We would play with hot ice. I begged and pleaded with my mom to allow me to go and play with the other children, but she would not budge. As a compromise she gave me permission to ride the school bus home with my classmates. Isn't it funny how as children we can be so hurt over something simple one minute and completely satisfied by something small the next? I was perfectly satisfied riding the school bus home in my best dress, after getting the prize, with my classmates. It made me so happy that I had forgotten all about the hot ice and sitting on a platform unable to play.

I had so much fun on the bus with my friends that I didn't notice Mrs. Cloise's broach had somehow fallen off of my blouse! We rushed back to catch up with the bus to try to find it but to no avail. Mom was so hurt when she had to tell her friend what had happened to the broach. Surprisingly she was more hurt than Mrs. Cloise, who just took it in stride and forgave. Years later I often thought of those simpler days and longed for life to be that easy again; for people to be so forgiving.

When I was in second grade I hated Fridays. Fridays were when we had spelling tests. The teacher would always hit me on my backside or on my hand for not passing the spelling test. Sometimes I would try very hard to pass the test and at other times I didn't try to pass at all. What was the sense? I got used to just pulling up my sweater and taking the licks. I'd cry for the moment and then move on. They were allowed to whip us as discipline because it was the South.

Other than school I loved growing up in the South. It was great to be able to go outside and just pick fresh fruit from the trees; peaches were my favorite. The smell of fresh cut grass was a delight to my nostrils throughout my childhood and going to church on Sundays was a tradition. People went to church with pride when I was growing up. Mom and dad would take my brother and I each week all year round. Winters were often cold, even in the South. I could remember all of us sitting around a big potbellied stove in the church. For years, it was the only source of heat. On holidays like Easter Sunday the children would have to memorize and recite a poem. Mom worked very hard to make sure that I knew my part. Of course, I always learned it very well.

Chapter 2

MOVING TO CONNECTICUT

We moved to Hartford, Connecticut in hopes of having a better life. Hartford was not exactly my dream home as a child, but it was the place to which I was transported from my beloved South. We rode on a bus all night long and it seemed as if we would never arrive at our destination. We finally got into a taxi that took us to the final location, our new home, where my dad was waiting for us. I was so glad to see my dad. We had not seen him for about a month because he had to search for a job and he was dearly missed. He was leading our family; even from a far distance and being reunited with him was very special.

The new house seemed so tall; especially to such a small girl. I had never seen "houses sitting on top of houses" before coming North. From the taxi window I could see that the ground was covered in white and I said to my mother,

"Mommy, look at all that cotton on the ground!"

In my mind I was thinking of how much money we could make gathering the cotton which was everywhere. The taxi driver laughed out loud and explained to me that it was something called snow. He described it as being cold and surely not cotton.

After exiting the taxi we gathered our things and ran up to the third floor to our new home in the sky. My brother and I were very happy to be reunited with our dad. It felt safe and right to be with him again. It also took some of the parenting load off of our mother. In the mornings my mom had to cook our breakfast over a hotplate because there was no stove or refrigerator in the house as of yet.

The following morning after my dad went to work, my mom, brother, and I went to the store down the street. We were unfamiliar with the area and had a great idea to count from the moment we left the house until we got to the store. We did the same thing when we returned. We knew when we arrived at that number that we had to be home. This kept us from getting lost in the middle of buildings that looked similar in unfamiliar neighborhoods. This was not like our home in the South where things were spread out and not so built up.

The first day of 4th grade was almost more than I could take. The school was so huge compared to the small school that I was used to. On top of that, the children were sometimes out of control. For the first time in my life I had a white teacher. There was one student in the classroom that did not obey anything that the teacher asked him to do. He always caused the teacher such great problems that she could not control the class. That day she took the unruly boy to the bathroom to wash his mouth out with soap for saying naughty things. Coming from the South, I could not understand why the teacher was having such a problem with one child! Why didn't she just take out a belt or paddle and spank the child as they did back home? The teachers in the South would not tolerate this kind of behavior. They would spank you and that would be that; pure and simple.

I made a friend named Kelly Lewis who lived in a bright pink house. It was the only pink house on the street. She and I became good friends. A week after becoming friends with her I met the Washington family who lived directly across the street from us. Who would have known that almost fifty years later the Washington family would play an important role in who I am today?

Mrs. Washington was a very good cook. Her specialty was spaghetti and meatballs. In order to do it just right she would start out early in the morning and cook the sauce all day. At about four or five in the afternoon family and friends would begin to gather. This was a typical Saturday for us and it made our childhood afternoons in Connecticut very special.

I watched the girls of that family, whom were my friends, grow up and leave for school with a purpose. Vickie was the oldest daughter. She and her sister Karen went off to college over the years. Even though Karen regularly stayed after school for dance class or something else, it was still a sentimental moment when she left home for good. But, I weathered the storm because her younger sister Donna was still home for me to have a playmate and close girlfriend in the same family.

Soon after, I met the White family. Gloria and I became the best of friends. Gloria and I were together every day. Each afternoon when school was out we would go to the Washington's house. I didn't like going to my house because there was always some kind of chore for me to do. I could never just come in and sit down with my friends at home like I could at their house.

In order to hang out with my friends I would get all of my stuff done before my mom returned from work. I had a cooking class at school and liked to try to cook everything I learned at home. I just had to make sure to clean up before mom returned. My mom would come home tired. Cooking was one of the only classes I loved, along with gym and sewing, so it was an important part of my day. I was able to test what I had learned and try new things that I could teach myself. If what I tried didn't come out right I would throw it away and try it again. I would get burnt out but then turn around and do the same thing the next day. I was determined to learn, even if it took some fussing and extreme patience to get it.

I'm sure my mom blessed the day that I started my sewing class at school. Instead of cooking everything daily I began sewing as much as I could. It wasn't unusual for me to have a new skirt or a pair of pants sewn before my mom could get home in the evening. I loved to sew just as much as I loved cooking. Besides, if I was sewing I wouldn't be in my mom's way when she was trying to cook. It was a beautiful balance to have in place.

I made some more new friends Coretha and Evette. Sometimes I would hang out with them. We learned how to make money for our church and we were all on the usher board. Believe it or not, I was actually the President for a number of years.

Baking and sewing took the place of my homework. I never wanted to do any other homework. Whenever my mom would ask if I had done my homework I would say yes. No one ever questioned if it was true. My mom was always doing chores around the house and working hard in order to get up very early the next morning for work. I would run across the street to my home away from home and like clockwork, my mom would call five minutes later. She'd be asking me to come home to do something. It got to the point where when the phone rang, without even answering it, Mrs. Washington would say,

"Irene is calling for Brenda."

I would go home to do what my mom asked and as soon as she turned her back I would run right back across the street. The Washington's home was always a safe place for me and other children to be. There was always someone to talk to there. If Karen was busy I would talk to her parents or perhaps her other sisters if they were home. You had to be respectful in order to be welcomed in their home. We could always do a lot of baking and no one seemed to care what we used. I never felt lonely when I was in their presence. I truly loved, respected and accepted them as my extended family.

Chapter 3

LOVE; THE JOY AND PAIN IT BRINGS

As a child, I had some serious problems when it came to school. It started in the South and continued when I moved North. I felt that school work was too hard for me and that I would never need what they were trying to teach me anyway. The only thing I thought I would need in life would be a husband and my own children. I didn't think of needing a job or having a profession. I really didn't think of myself as qualified to do anything but be a wife and a mother. I was okay with being a stay at home mom, or working in a factory if I had to work outside of my home. I was content with work that wouldn't require an education.

No one in my immediate family had ever finished high school. The small amount I had learned was alright with my parents and I. College just seemed so farfetched for me to ever attend, let alone graduate. The only person in my whole family that I knew went to college was my Aunt Chris. I never even knew what it took to go to college. I just honestly felt like it was not for me and that I was never going to get there. Besides, I thought people had to be really smart to go to college. Smart, I was not and I was completely okay with that.

When I came up North the hitting days at school were over; or so I thought. You see, I met one of my 6th grade teachers at Northwest Jones. That teacher reminded me of the Southern teaching method all over again. He would have me stick out my hand and strike it with a wooden paddle. If the kids in class would misbehave he would have the whole class walk up and down the stairway until we were so tired. If you stopped you would get another swat on the hand. For a season I felt the South…

In 6th grade I won the best dressed award. It was the only award I had ever won. In 7th grade a new boy came to our school in the middle of the year. His name was Keith and he was my first crush. We talked a little bit, but this other girl liked him too. At the end of 7th grade he went back to Barber Street School. My first crush had suddenly disappeared into thin air.

8th grade was when my brother started drinking. My brother's friends would bring him home at 8 a.m. in the morning before school even started. They would ring the doorbell and take off and run after they heard my father come to the door. He would look at my dad and say,

"Are you mad at me?"

My father knew he was too intoxicated so he wouldn't say anything. Instead, he would just put him in the bed. Then on the next day he would talk to him. I never knew he was an alcoholic until he drank a whole fifth of alcohol by himself and was still standing. To witness this with own eyes was horrific in its own right.

By the ninth grade Gloria and I spent much of our time in the halls. I would at least try to catch up on some of my school work when I did attend a class, but this wasn't too often. I had a few teachers that would try to get me to attend class some of the time and show me the value of an education. But, I didn't always listen.

Then I started business class and I found something else to love in school. While in that class I began to think that maybe I could do business in the world but that thought did not last too long. My self esteem was too low and I just couldn't muster up strength to believe in myself.

REUNITED WITH KEITH

While in the ninth grade I got myself a boyfriend. It was the same boy from 7th grade who was my first crush. He was my first real boyfriend. He never asked me out officially; we just started dating. At this point I stopped spending all of my time with Gloria and spent most of my time with Keith. All of the girls were crazy about Keith. He was good looking, slightly bowlegged with slanted eyes and was everything I ever wanted in a boyfriend.

Every chance I got Gloria and I would ride our bikes to the end of town. This would allow me to see Keith. My parents didn't allow me to have a boyfriend at my age so everything we did had to be sneaky so they wouldn't find out. Gloria was the only person that knew everything about me. I remember telling her when Keith asked me to have sex with him and I said no. I didn't want that from him at that point in my life so I kept saying no. All I wanted was the same thing that most girls wanted back then; a good-looking boyfriend.

Keith waited patiently for me to say yes to have sex with him. I could tell though that his patience was running out. I did not want to lose him. I really liked him and thought it was love. One day we were at my mother's house and we were sitting on the sofa. Nobody was home but us. I ended up saying yes to have sex with Keith. I had no idea what to expect about sex.

We got in my bed which had pink sheets. He took the lead and I just held on to him for dear life. It was very, very painful. After it was over I knew I had to get rid of the sheets. I waited until Keith left and threw them out in the garbage. Luckily my mother never asked for those pink sheets again. After having sex with Keith I felt a new closeness and strengthened bond with him. I felt that we really belonged together. I think I was the first virgin that Keith had been with. It was a bond that I thought would not and could not be broken. We seemed destined to be united forever.

From that day on we were together every single day. We would leave school to go to my house and have sex at 12:30p.m. and then go back to school. After school was dismissed we would go back to my house again. We had this schedule down pact. We seemed inseparable.

One day at the end of 9th grade we were innocently talking together. I thought it was going well, but his mind went in another direction. I didn't have a clue that this would be the last time I would see or talk to him again for a while. He was the love of my life and like most girls with a deep crush I called or looked for him every day for weeks. His mother did not tell me that he was gone. I rode my bike daily to the other end of town, as Gloria and I always did, just to get a glance of him. But, he was not around. I did not understand. Why wouldn't he call me?

Finally, after a month of phone calls, his mother told me that Keith had run away from home. I was devastated! I moved on with my life with the thought in the back of my mind that I would surely see him again one day.

After a while, Keith began to call me on the phone every night. And then he stopped calling me again and I lost contact with him for three months. When he finally called again he explained that the reason he wasn't in touch with me. He said that he had been shot three times, stabbed and left for dead. He was in the hospital for months recuperating and they didn't know who he was because he didn't have an ID on him. The pain in his voice broke my heart. To know the love of my life had been secretly suffering and I had no clue put a heavy weight on my soul. We talked more little by little until Keith disappeared once again.

This was close to the same time that the Dowdell family moved next door to us on Deerfield Avenue. Now I had a new safe place to hang out. Ms. Dowdell had five girls and each one planted a seed in my heart over the years. I was happy to be living next door to them. They would play a great role in my life from that time onward.

ANOTHER NEW BOYFRIEND

I made friends with another family that also lived on Deerfield Avenue. A girl named Carol and I became friends. Carol always seemed to be so mean yet we forged a friendship. I also befriended her cousin, Cornell, who became the second guy my mom would allow me to see. I began to date him since I thought the relationship between Keith and I was completely over. He would come over and sit in the living room with me. He was also older than me. We became very close and we were in a relationship as boyfriend and girlfriend. He never tried to have sex with me; not even once. It was my first relationship without sex. He took me to his senior prom and I was the youngest person there as a sophomore.

I now know that he would have made a good husband for me. This is one of the things that convinced me. Even though I had a lot of hair he knew I loved hair pieces and wigs. On one of his visits he brought me a beautiful hairpiece. I was so happy that he thought enough about me to bring me that hairpiece. How many men do you know will do this? I also loved his grandmother. She wanted us to get married because she thought we were so good for each other. I loved his entire family. They were very nice to me. He was definitely a man I envisioned being with.

LONG DISTANCE BUT STILL CLOSE

After my entire sophomore year went by, my ex-boyfriend Keith called me on the phone and informed me that he was secretly coming into town. He told me that I could tell no one. Of course I took it that meant no one else but Gloria. But, I had to tell her! This was too exciting to keep to myself. The day that he was to come I went to school in the morning and left early to go home and wait for him at 12:30 p.m. I got all dressed up to see him because we had not seen each other for a year. I waited that entire afternoon, but Keith did not come. I just knew he had changed his mind about coming to town. I was sure if he had come to town that he would have called me to say that he was on his way.

At about 6:00 p.m., after my parents had returned, I heard the door-bell ring. My heart pounded as I ran to the door and saw that it was him. However, behind the great happiness came shock and disappointment. It was Keith alright, but he did not come alone. He had another female with him. I was in utter shock and didn't know what to say to him; let alone what to think. At that moment I knew any relationship we had was over. When Keith and I were alone in the living room he told me that this girl was his prostitute and she meant nothing to him.

Keith proceeded to tell me about his life since the time he had left home. He said he was tired of his mother always trying to tell him what to do. In turn, he decided to run away and take a bus to New York City. He could no longer stay in Connecticut because his mom worked for the local police department and his brother was also a sergeant on the police force. He shared that he dealt with a lot of prostitutes in New York and informed me that they were much older than him. He then left New York and moved to Washington, D.C. He never told me why he left New York.

He told me that after being in D.C. for a while he had been shot and stabbed. He said he was hospitalized for three months and nearly died. He explained that this was the reason he did not call me.

They stayed and visited with me for about two hours before leaving for the hotel. They needed to rest in preparation to go to D.C. in the morning. I was so hurt… there were no words to describe it. I tried really hard to keep myself together, but Keith knew that this would hurt me and that was why he didn't show up at 12:30 p.m. that afternoon. 12:30 p.m. was our special time because that was when we usually had sex. He missed it on purpose because he knew we couldn't have sex while my parents were home and he also didn't want to hurt me anymore; especially since he was already with another woman.

From that time onward he would call me often just to talk. I was so happy every time he called because it proved he had not forgotten about me. His family didn't find out that he had been in town until weeks later. It was so good to see him. I thought that the handwriting was on the wall for our relationship. Was I naive? Perhaps; but I loved him deeply.

THE PAST BECOMES PRESENT

One ruinous day I received another call from Keith. He said that he was on his way back into town; this time to stay. He would be there by that evening and wanted to see me. I thought that my prayers had been answered. I was very excited and happy, but a little sad as well. I knew that if Keith was back in my life then I would not be able to see Cornell any more.

When Keith came back at the end of 11th grade it was as if he never left. We were together once again. Whatever Cornell and I had was over. One Saturday afternoon Keith and I were sitting on the side of the school on a bench. It was just the two of us. I looked up and there was Cornell walking by. He looked over at me and our eyes met. I could see the hurt in his eyes because he had no idea that Keith was back in my life as my man. I was so sad that I hurt him. I never talked to him again until a couple of years later. We never talked about that day and how deep I had hurt his feelings. All I knew was that the love of my life Keith was back and we were together again.

I remember early one morning sitting in the high school cafeteria with Gloria and Keith before class. Suddenly Gloria got into a fight with another girl. She picked her up and threw her across the table. Keith and I had to break up the fight before anyone got in trouble for it. I felt like we were already in enough trouble.

On another day, a girl that liked Keith brushed up against me at school and we fought. Gloria was right there in the fight with me after she saw that I was losing. All three of us were taken to the office. I thought the other girl was still in the office next to ours with school officials until the police came to ask us questions about Keith. They were trying to find out if we knew where he was. It turned out that the office had let the girl leave early and had forgotten that Keith was right outside of the school waiting. When he saw the girl he hit her in the head with a two-by-four piece of wood. His anger and rage to protect me lead to this unfortunate decision he made.

I wish that had been the end of this drama, but sadly it was not. After a couple of days of out of school suspension we returned to school only to have all four of us fight again! We were all expelled, which forced our parents to find other schools to send us to. I went to Hartford High for the rest of my junior year.

My relationship with Keith got much deeper and closer. We were always together after school at this time. He and I loved to dress alike and have photo shoots at Lauren Studios. That was the popular place in the area to have photos taken during this time. They would blow some of them up poster size and put them on display each time we would go there.

Ms. Dowdell, my next door neighbor, told me to ask my parents for birth control pills because she knew I was having sex. Her five daughters were very open with her, so I confided in her as well. I finally got the courage to ask my parents for the birth control pills, but they said no. They thought that they would be giving me permission to have sex by doing so.

At age 16 I got pregnant and was carrying Keith's baby. I was terrified to tell my parents. I told my mom and she told my dad. They got together and decided that I wasn't going to have the baby. They called the doctor and everything to set up the abortion process. I disagreed and told my parents that I wasn't going to have an abortion.

When it came time to have the abortion the doctor was at the hospital waiting for me and called my house to ask why I was late. My dad told him that I had a change of mind and I wasn't going to proceed. The doctor wanted me to go there anyway. My dad gave me the phone and the doctor started asking me questions.

"How are you going to take care of a baby at 16?"

Hearing the doctor's perspective influenced me greatly. I gave in and decided to have the abortion right then and there since everything was already set up. I didn't have time to call Keith and tell him. I just did it...

Keith knew and understood that I liked nice things and tried to give me as much as possible. This was done while in high school and after. My mom allowed him to give me gifts only on special occasions such as birthdays and Christmas. I remember one time when he purchased a television console from G Fox and Company for me. But, when they attempted to deliver it my parents told them to take it back. I was not allowed to receive expensive gifts like that from a boy so young. I was so angry! However, the day of the Super Bowl that year my dad's television broke. He asked me if Keith still had the gift he tried to give me. If so, he gave him permission to bring it back that day.

Keith was always asking my parents if he could marry me. His family, on the other hand, wanted him to marry a judge's daughter who lived in a large yellow house that sat on top of a hill. Keith did not want to marry her. I also did not like the fact that his family did not approve of me. This was very bothersome to me.

I began smoking cigarettes at the age of 17. I can remember lying on a white shag rug on the floor in Keith's mother's house. The fire place was burning eloquently. Keith lit a cigarette and it enticed me. He looked so appealing smoking and I asked him to teach me how to smoke and he did. He definitely had a strong influence over me in a major way. I honestly was truly in love with him.

At age 17 I got pregnant again. I remember being so happy to be pregnant with the child of the man I loved and desired to marry. I was excited that I had to tell my closest friends. Ms. Washington told me that I had to tell my parents myself. She said that they deserved the respect to hear it from me and not anyone else. My mom was very hurt and unkind upon hearing the news. She used the situation to lash out and call me cruel names. When she went into another room I ran from her house. I had made up my mind that I was going to run away with the love of my life. I refused to let her, any person or anything else deter me from doing so.

I figured out how to get enough money to take a taxi to Keith's work place. I ran to Karen and Donna's house and they scraped up some money for me. I had to wait for him to get off of work. At the time Keith worked in a restaurant. He no longer lived with his mom. He rented a room at a local rooming house. While at his job I looked out of the window just in time to see the green car with the white top pull up. I tried my best to hide because I recognized that it was my mom's car! She had called Donna and Karen. As usual they told on me. They told her that I had gone to the restaurant where Keith worked. Even though my mom knew where he worked she always wanted Karen or Donna to ride with her.

My mom saw me and gave me no choice but to crowd into the car with her and my friends. The ride back seemed to take forever. The car was as quiet as a tomb. Once we arrived and went into the house no one spoke a word. Two quiet days seemed like an eternity until my parents finally decided to break the silence. They had decided that Keith and I should be married. After all, Keith had been asking them to allow me to marry him for a while. There was no better time than now. I later learned that they did not want people to gossip about me saying I was pregnant and unmarried. I also felt that people would look at them as though they were not good parents because they had a 17 year old daughter pregnant and unmarried. What they really did was give me permission and a license to have sex.

MARRIAGE

My future husband and I were talking on the phone the night before we were to be married. He called to tell me that he did not want to get married after all. I never thought that he didn't love me. I now know that he loved me more than I knew he did. I know that in his heart, he was not ready to settle down with one woman. He knew in his heart that he wanted to continue with the lifestyle he had been living while in Washington D.C. I began to tell him,

"How can you do this to me? Everyone is going to be expecting a wedding."

Keith was telling me in his own words that he loved me, but he had changed. Thinking back over the situation now I know that the relationship should have been over the day he came to visit me from Washington D.C. with the woman. Keith enjoyed living the life of a pimp. He loved the excitement and thrill of controlling different women and making money while doing so.

Just as I turned 3 ½ months pregnant I ended up marrying my love in my parent's living room; white dress and all. He had a change of heart and vowed to marry me and he did. I was 18 years old. Karen was my maid of honor and my other friend Gail played the traditional song - *Here Comes the Bride*. The pastor from our church married us and the room was filled with friends and family members on both sides. I don't remember my brother being there for this special occasion.

I'll never forget the rain. It poured furiously on the day we got married. Was this a sign that this marriage was never to be and would never work? I should have taken it as a sign. Nonetheless, we held hands and jumped into his brother's brown and beige Cadillac and rode to the reception. We were happily in love and weren't going to allow the rain to ruin our moment.

The reception was at an event hall that was owned by relatives of the Washington family. Our honeymoon was at the Holiday Inn in Hartford, CT. For me it didn't really matter where we went on our honeymoon. I was just happy to be married to him. My friend Vickie asked,

"What are you guys going to do on your honeymoon night; watch TV?"

While laughing snidely… It didn't even faze me much because I was content just to be close to and openly married to my love.

NEWLYWEDS

The next day we went straight back to the apartment that Keith and I had found a month before and furnished it. It was in January and the weather was bitter cold. The heater had broken and the cold was unbearable. We could only stay one night. We went back to my parent's house to stay. I thought we would be able to get the Landlord to repair the heater, but he would not. We moved our things out quickly and remained with my parents from January to April. Keith loved decorating the apartment as much as I did however he was out of the house more than he was there. Keith and I had stopped doing things together as we always had been. That's when I knew there was someone else in the picture other than me. His attitude and mannerisms had changed big time. I realized at that point I shouldn't have gotten married… but it was too late.

One night no one was home but Keith and I. Keith had dropped my mother and father off at a birthday party. I was nine months pregnant at this time. I started talking to Keith about him never being home with me. With no hesitation he slapped me in my face and said,

"Your face isn't pregnant."

I was in shock. That was the first sign of abusiveness and I should've walked out then and there. I was so hurt that he would hit me while I was nine months pregnant. I was so emotionally and physically hurt that I just went to sleep. The next day I acted like nothing happened. The relationship should have been over that day because once a man hits you once he will surely hit you again. The abuse is only going to get worse once you marry an abuser.

He never knew his own father because he was never in his life. He also never knew his biological mother until 3 months after we were married. He was adopted at a young age. He stumbled upon meeting his family through a young lady that he was trying to get to be his prostitute. She had been a prostitute for years and was older than him. It turned out that the young girl he was trying to put on "*ho stroll*" was his own sister! His entire family always knew who he was and where he was, but they were not allowed to tell him who they were. His sister decided it was time to tell him who she was in the hopes that he would stop trying to put her on the street. She took him to meet his birth mother and his siblings. Keith began spending much of his time over at their house in attempt to get to know them.

We then moved from the first floor of my mother's apartment to the third floor. We fixed it up extravagantly. Keith was paying the rent with his pimp and hustling money. He paid all of the bills. Unlike some couples, we moved in with a house that was fully furnished. My husband even surprised me with the matching console record player that matched the television. He loved to surprise me with gifts. After two weeks in that house it looked as if it was mine. I was so proud of it and how much I loved Keith.

RAIN SOMETIMES FALLS IN TEARS

Before I delivered my son I was always at home; looking out of the window crying. I cried while looking for my husband to come down the street. Oh, I tried to be strong. I didn't want anyone else to see my tears, but each night I cried myself to sleep. The pain was too much. It was too much to know that I had a husband that just stopped coming home to me at night. No one had to tell me that I had made a huge mistake. I knew I made the wrong choice in him and that I used to have it made living with my parents. At home I didn't have to do anything but go to school, do homework, help with housework, and obey my parent's rules. I had gotten what I longed for with Keith, but I had no idea how much pain it would bring into my life to have it.

It was coming close to the graduation of my senior class. I paid for my cap and gown and trusted that I would still be able to graduate with them after I had my baby. I hoped to graduate, but reality set in. I knew at that point that my life was changing…forever.

Chapter 4

TROUBLE IN PARADISE LOST

What happened? My world was spinning upside down and out of control. Where was that pretty little girl that loved to cook over the rocks in her playhouse to receive the praises from her daddy? Where were the lazy days of summer on the farm and the beauty of the Southern fields white with cotton? All of that seemed a million miles away. I felt so lost and so alone.

I would cry and cry night after night until I could not stay awake any longer. The night I went into labor my wayward husband took me to the hospital, however the hospital sent us back home. Hours later the pain was so bad we went back. I remember being in so much pain that all I could do is cry and rest my head on his shoulder. Finally, they came and called me into the delivery room by myself. My husband was not allowed. The pain was terrible and would not stop. I was all alone. The doctor soon came in and told me that I needed to have a caesarian section. This required the signature of my husband, but by then he was nowhere to be found. He had waited as long as he could and left before he knew that I needed surgery. I gave the doctor a number to call my mother. The doctors called her and she came immediately to sign the papers for the C-section. My baby boy was born on a Tuesday at 2:09 p.m. in June of 1975. When I awakened the first person I saw was my smiling mother. She told me I had give birth to a boy. I asked her if he was healthy and if he had hair on his head. She answered yes to both questions. I fell back into an exhausted sleep and awakened when my husband came at 8:00 p.m. From then on Keith was there every night until they would put him out. Several times he hid in the closet to stay longer. I was there for six days in all.

Here was the problem. I gave birth and came home from the hospital with my beautiful new son in my arms. This took place the day before the graduation ceremony. The day I came home my husband didn't even know that I had been released from the hospital until much later. My mother took me to her home and cared for the baby and I. All of my friends came by to see my new baby. My husband named him Keith Anthony Martin, Jr. He won the right because we made a deal that if it was a boy, he could name him; if it was a girl then I could name her. I was so certain it was going to be a girl.

Keith came home that morning about 1:00 a.m. He put our son on his chest and fell asleep exhausted. Keith Jr actually fell off of his father's chest. Luckily his father caught him by his legs, which kept him from hitting the hardwood floor!

EVIL SPIRITS REAPPEAR

A few days later we returned to our upstairs apartment. It was a hot summer day in June and very uncomfortable for me and my newborn. About ten days into being new parents my husband came home with a friend. I was glad to see him because I desperately needed help. I asked him to take me to the Laundromat because the laundry was stacked up in the house and I was unable to wash it due to caring for our baby by myself. He boldly said no in front of his friend who was in our house. I was so angry with him for just walking away. He knew how badly I needed to wash clothes. Then, suddenly it happened. Unexpectedly, he shoved his fist into my face with great force. In defense, I took a stand-up ashtray and struck him. He then threw me to the floor, near the couch, where my baby was laying. I was so afraid that my son would be hurt, but someone came into the room and grabbed my son. They took him into another room. My husband continued punching me recklessly and nonstop. I vulnerably pleaded with him to stop many times but he did not until he was ready. Like a villain who carries no remorse, he simply walked off into another room.

Everything went crazy in that moment for me. I stood up, picked up the tall ashtray again, followed and hit Keith in the head with it. In a moment of insanity and utter chaos he swiftly picked up our son and left our house. Can you imagine being beaten unexpectedly by your own husband? Can you imagine the pierce suffering my heart experienced as I helplessly watched him take our newborn son and leave?

I was entering into the most difficult season of my simple life. My husband had taken my son and left the house. I fell to the floor crying; not knowing what to do. My face was so swollen but it didn't compare to the painful fact that he took my baby from me.

I rushed next door to ask Ms. Dowell to take me to look for my son. She was very concerned when she saw how bruised I was. She took me in her vehicle, in spite of my agony, to search for my baby. We went to a few places that I thought he might go. Unfortunately, we found no help. It was only then that I decided to go to another friend's house. There DeeDee was sitting outside on the porch holding a pillow. I jumped out hastily and asked her what she was holding. I heard her welcoming response,

"Your baby."

At first I didn't want to believe that she was holding my baby on that pillow. I ran from the car and took my son into my arms and held him. I kissed his precious little face over and over again. As she went into her house to get his bag, Keith appeared from nowhere. The anger in his eyes terrified me so much that my body froze. He angrily took my baby out of my arms and walked away with him for a second time. I returned to our housebroken and defeated.

FOOLS GOLD

Soon after I returned home my husband returned with my son. He was quiet for a while. He then looked into my face and spoke these words:

"I'm so sorry. I promise you this will never happen again. I just want you to be okay."

I believed him; as most abused people do at first. You want it to be true so badly that you believe. You just believe they are telling the truth that you want and need to hear. In that moment I was not looking at what had happened, nor was I looking at the rage that had been on his face. I was reminiscing on all of the good years and times we had experienced together. I looked at all of the times that he protected me by not allowing anyone to touch me. I could hear him asking my mom and dad over and over again to allow him to marry me. I then could see all of the things he promised that our marriage would be like. I married him at 18 years old because I loved him and felt that he loved me so much. I was so happy to be the wife of Keith A. Martin, also known as, the love of my life. My dream had come true and I had just turned 18 ten days before then. Ours would be a great marriage; a loving one. Together we could conquer the world. We would teach our son how to work hard and we would have that white picket fence and every other happiness that came with it.

For the most part Keith always said that I was his *main lady* and his wife. He tried to keep me away from being involved with his street life. I tried to be the perfect wife. I would cook, clean and care for our baby. But, what was supposed to be the beginning of a lifetime of love and happiness (*til death do us part*) became a cycle of running for my life! I had been pregnant and all alone; often crying for him to come home. Deep inside, I knew from the first day of the marriage that this was not meant to be and that it would never work. This was the beginning of a long life of disappointments and pain.

My mind went back to the day that I first entered into that third floor house; the one Keith and I then called home. It was when I was but a little girl who just arrived from the South with my family. The building looked so tall back then and everything was so new. I was just an innocent girl living there and making friends. Now I felt as though that place had become my prison. I had been a pregnant prisoner. I was destined and doomed to look out of the bedroom window with a face full of tears. I was desperately looking for a sign that he was coming home to me. I would leave the bedroom window and go to the living room window. I would look long and hard hoping to see him. This was what I would do until three or four a.m. in the morning. I did this until I just couldn't stay awake any longer. This was my routine night after night. When he did finally come home I would make love to him just like nothing was wrong. Looking back, I can't believe I would do that. Even worse, I would do the same thing hours after he would beat me up! The next day I shoved the beating aside and acted like nothing had happened the night before.

When we got married my mom gave us a pretty round, blue, velvet bed. It was extravagant like the kind they gave as a prize on the TV show *The Price is Right*. Keith and his friends would always come over and spread stolen money on top of that bed to count it. It was like something you would watch on television or in a movie.

YOU CAN RUN, BUT YOU CANNOT HIDE

One day when I was home alone I heard the doorbell ring. When I answered it was Keith's brother. He was a police sergeant. As I stuck my head out, I could see that the entire building was surrounded by undercover police officers and FBI agents. As it turns out my husband was wanted for a bank robbery.

My brother-in-law asked me if Keith was at home and I answered truthfully,

"No."

They then went into our house and searched it from top to bottom. Can you imagine being an 18 year old newlywed and having this happen? I was being interrogated daily for a period of time.

I started working at Stanadyne as a machine operator full time. My brother also worked there. I was very happy to get a real job that paid good money. Sadly, my mind was still in a terrible place. This life that was supposed to be a happy one was now my greatest nightmare. I have memories of being forced to be the driver of his Cadillac as his prostitutes sat in the back seat. There was a time when we were supposed to be going to a concert, but we never made it there. One time I told Keith that I was not going anywhere with him and his prostitutes. He struck me so hard! I jumped out of the car and ran to a friend's house to hide. When I thought he was gone I ran home and called the police. He was there when they came and they cuffed him. He was going to be arrested but I asked them not to do it out of fear. He arrogantly told the police that they should never come to arrest him if I called. He said I would never have him arrested and truthfully he was right. I was so angry and I wanted to tell them to take him this time but I did not. Fear is a terrible prison guard.

Just after the police left I walked back into the house. I was followed by my very angry husband. He stood in the middle of the living room floor and grabbed me. He cut my outfit off of me with a straight razor. That razor could have easily been my throat. I was terrified and afraid to cry out; much less move. Right then I heard my father pulling into the driveway. I waited until I could hear him get out of the car and yelled as loud as I could out of one of the third floor windows. My father knew that we were fighting again and called out for me, but I was too afraid to answer. He swiftly came upstairs to our apartment. When he saw the look on my face he asked me to come downstairs with him. We called the police for the second time that night. This time they sent five policemen. One of them was the lieutenant who came out to see why they had been called to the same residence twice in the same night with no arrest. When the officers started to go up the stairs they heard a lot of dogs barking loudly. They came back down and asked me to go up first. I told them that I would not have called them if I was not afraid also!

Suddenly, a door opened to the upstairs and Keith came out with five dogs. He had dogs that usually stayed outside. The officers grabbed him and a fight broke out. It spilled out into the first floor. One officer began to choke my husband with a police stick. This overwhelmed my dad. He then moved in on Keith and held him down so the authorities could handcuff him. Like a scene out of a movie, Keith turned over and karate kicked one of the officers in the nose. He was still dangerous even when handcuffed. They arrested him this time without any hesitation because now they had a reason; assault on an officer.

IMPRISONED BUT NOT RESTRICTED

In our area we had a street similar to streets in other cities. These streets were filled with prostitutes who hunted for Johns. Johns were men who paid prostitutes for sexual services. We called that area in slang language "ho (short for whore) stroll". The day after Keith was arrested I proudly drove his brown Cadillac up and down that street. His prostitutes were so angry with me that they yelled and cursed at me for having him arrested. They scolded me for having the nerve to drive his car on their street.

A day later I actually drove to the police department. How I got upstairs into the jail area where male inmates were being held is still a mystery to me. I went to visit my husband. Somehow we could talk to each other but we couldn't see each other. Of course he started out with a big apology. Yes, it was the same apology that I had fallen for before. This was just prison talk but I still foolishly believed him yet again. I went to court with him and told the judge something like,

"Your honor, he didn't mean it."

Unfortunately, it worked and the judge released him after about two days. People use the phrase, "This is the beginning of the end." From my heart I know that this thing that began with us just wouldn't seem to end. Truthfully, it should have never begun.

Chapter 5

HELL DOES HAVE FURY

They say that hell has no fury like a woman scorned. I have lived to see that this is not true of all scorned women. Some of us are just too fearful to defend ourselves or we have no real sense of direction to find ourselves. I was caught in a nightmare that started out as the dream of a lifetime. Bad behavior from Keith became the norm and was primarily expected. Good behavior from Keith was a welcomed surprise when it came. This was not a marriage made in heaven. Instead, it was a prison born in hell. The worst part about it is that everything was not all bad all of the time. When it was bad, it was unbearably bad. Now all I had was my tears to comfort me until I found something greater. Or should I say *someone* greater than my despair.

They say, "Sauce for the goose is the same for the gander." I was willing to start proving that it was true. Keith was trying to get a certain prostitute to start working for him and he was always in her house. One day I gave her a call and asked her to make sure he stayed there because her boyfriend was at my house. I only knew her boyfriend because I used to model with him years earlier. Keith got so angry that he came over to our apartment and broke the door down. I guess I had gotten so tired of playing his game that I thought I'd try one of my own. It didn't seem to work. He still did whatever he wanted to do as if nothing I said or did mattered at all.

One day my husband gave me the car to take the baby to the doctor. When I returned from the doctor holding my little one I saw a scene that was unbelievable. My husband had taken the time while I was gone to bring red paint into our attic apartment. On the white slanted attic wall he wrote the words whore and bitch." He wrote them in huge letters. This was when my baby was about 5 months old. His disrespect of me considered to grow immeasurably.

Thinking that I couldn't win I decided to have an affair with an old classmate named Sean. We had become sex partners. When Keith wasn't home Sean would come over in the middle of the night after the clubs had closed. We had sex and then he went home because he was married. This went on for several years.

I had a lifestyle of running from Keith. My faithful friend Gloria and I were running for cover from that angry man. Keith would just let it rip for no reason at all. Many times I had to run to one of my girlfriend's homes in my bathrobe and slippers just to escape his anger. He would cut up photos, break things in the house, cut the doorbell wires, and too often punch and kick holes in the walls.

ROBBERY UP CLOSE AND PERSONAL

One night while I was at work I got a frantic phone call from my mom. She said that Keith had rented a U-Haul truck and was moving everything out of the house. That man took everything out of the house but a few things. We had two silverware sets and he didn't even leave one for me. My mom stood on the steps of the house with a butcher's knife in her hand and told him she was glad he was leaving but dared him to take that pretty round bed. She reminded him of the fact that she had bought that bed and it was going to stay with her! I guess he figured she wasn't operating with a full deck at that point and left that bed behind. He moved to one of his mother's properties.

When I finally got to the apartment I was so hurt that I just sat and cried. I couldn't imagine how he could do this to his son and I. Everything!

He really took everything! When I spoke to my attorney I recall him asking me if I wanted my furniture back and I said,

"No. Just like I got that furniture I will get more on my own that is even better."

I didn't divorce him then, but I should have done so. This man was not going to be a real father to his son. If he could wipe out everything from our home leaving nothing for his son, then what else could he do?

JUST WHAT WOULD HE DO NEXT?

One time I went with Gloria to the apartment of one of her friends. My car was parked outside on the street. All of a sudden we began to hear a horn blowing noisily and it would not stop. I looked out of the window and found that it was Keith. When I went down the stairs to the car he pulled out a gun and put it to my head. I was sure he was going to kill me that day but he didn't. That was the closest I had ever been to a gun in my life. When I didn't return up stairs right away, Gloria came down to check on me. She slowly approached the car and he put the gun to her head maliciously as well. In seeing the fear in our eyes he just laughed and laughed like a crazy man. What a terrible thing to do. What happened to the man I thought I had married?

His violence was getting worse and the fear was more than I could handle. This man would find my car and break out the windows. He was threatening me and was always around. I knew that I needed to become strong enough to get away from him and get out of this life. I couldn't get the police to stop him from breaking the windows on the car. Their argument was that the car was as much his as it was mine; citing that we were still married. They also told me something really frightening. They said if he came and took our son away they could not stop him or make him return my son because it was his son too. At that moment I knew I had to walk away.

This is when I filed for divorce because I didn't want him to take my two year old son. I didn't need his signature on the document. They just served him the paper. I went to court and I tried to get child support, but to no avail because he never had a legal job. His profession as a strip pimp was his only means of income. He never showed up in court and I never received child support.

I worked as best I could and saved my money to get an apartment for little Keith and I. I moved to Bowls Park because it was low income housing. It is sad to say that even after I divorced him and moved away that he was still in and out of my life. I would continuously fall for his lies and take him back over and over again. I would even go and visit him. While I would not allow him to live with us anymore I still slept with him. Regretfully, I still loved him.

Keith went to jail for 10 days and when he got out he came to live with me again. I let him come back because I was still in love and I was hoping it would work this time. I ended up getting pregnant again, but I knew I couldn't have this baby. I knew my mother wasn't going to help with this one. My only option was to have an abortion. I went to have the abortion done by myself. Soon after Keith moved out and back to his place. However, he would still come visit me.

Finally, I became strong enough to tell him on one of his many visits that I didn't want to see him anymore. He left the house, got in his car, and thought about my words. I heard the knock on the door and assumed he was back. I opened it to my own harm. He pulled back and punched me in the face with such force that I went flying across the room. My precious little son was standing there watching. He was about four years old. He started to cry and wouldn't leave from underneath me. I was conscious enough to grab my son and hold him tight. I was so angered with myself for allowing my son to be put in harm's way yet again.

MOVING ON

For a couple years I was by myself. I would stay home, work, cook, decorate and take care of my son. My girlfriends would always tell me to stop staying home so much and go out. One fateful night I went to a local bowling alley with a girlfriend. We met two guys and bowled with them all night long. The four of us had been drinking and I became so drunk that they brought me home and left me there with one of the guys. My friend had left with the other one. I remembered taking a bath, having sex, and going to bed with him. When I woke up I was startled and asked,

"Who is this ugly man in my bed?"

I told him he had to leave, as though I had no part in his being there to begin with.

This began a cycle of going out from time to time binge drinking. Literally every time I would go out I would get drunk. My mom always looked after baby Keith when I went out. This went on for another couple of years. It didn't take much for me to get drunk. Since I was not good at drinking I always got sick. With each time I would cry out to God to help me get better and I would promise Him that if He made me better I would never do it again. Just like a drunk, two or three weeks later, I would go out and do it all over again. In turn I would begin making the same lame promise to the Lord. I even tried smoking marijuana, but I didn't like the way it made me feel. I felt paranoid and couldn't move. It made feel on the edge as if someone was talking badly about me.

HOW DID I GET HERE?

One day when I was working at Stanadyne, two co-workers dropped by my house after work and offered me what they said was marijuana to smoke. I don't really know why I tried it because I did not like marijuana. I began to feel like I was floating. I was so light on my feet. I should have figured out that something was terribly wrong with this because the guys were not smoking what they gave to me.

They laughed at me and eventually left, but I wanted to talk to them or somebody. My son was outside giving candy and sweets to some of his friends. My neighbor was not home and I thought to myself that there was no one to talk to. So, eventually I called my mom. Once I got her on the phone I began to tell her things that I would never have told her if I were sober. She knew something was wrong and immediately came to get my son and I. She put me to bed and I slept the rest of the night until the following morning. When I woke up my father told me that he did not know what type of drugs I had, but demanded that I never have it again. I found out later that I had not just smoked marijuana, but the joint had been laced with *angel dust* or *PCP*. It was a hallucinogenic street drug that is highly addictive.

Chapter 6

NEW BEGINNINGS, SO IT SEEMED

A new man Devon entered my life. I met him at a nightclub called Main and Tower. He started coming by and spending time with me. This man was always polite and got along well with my son, which was the most important thing to me. I felt this was someone I wanted to spend the rest of my life with. We spent a lot of time together and I would love for him to cook for us. He was a really good cook. Pretty soon he moved into my apartment and we ended up living together for about six or seven years. After five years we had gotten engaged.

How that man loved to drink Hennessey, Courvoisier, and Remy Martin. These were his drinks and soon they became my favorite drinks too. I'm afraid that I was so in love with him that I could not see who he really was from the beginning. I couldn't see that he had a serious drinking problem. I never saw anything wrong with his drinking, even though most days he would pass out. I just was happy that he was fun when he woke up.

He began to drink more and more. It got to the point that he would be so drunk where you couldn't understand a single word he was saying. You could forget about his trying to walk, too! That was not going to happen. He had a good job doing construction for at least a couple of years that we were together. He was very talented despite the drinking problem he had.

A FAMILIAR SPIRIT SHOWS IT'S FACE

During our time together we drove two cars all the way to Alabama. We continued to Georgia and then South Carolina. Along the way we each had a gallon of Hennessey. When the bottles would get low we would just get more. At the time it did not matter to me because I did not have to drive at all. My boyfriend, Devon, liked to drive just as much as he liked to cook and drink.

By the time we reached Georgia we started to fight. Devon and his friend went out and I and my friend, Betty, went out shopping. We were supposed to meet up to go to the club. While me and Betty were getting ready Devon and his friend came back and said they weren't letting anymore people in the club. That was the best excuse they could come up with because they had already met some girls in the club. They wanted to go back to the club without us to meet up with the girls, but I told him he wasn't taking my car. He tried to take the keys anyway and that is when we fought. The next morning we all got in the car and drove to South Carolina, which was Devon's hometown. Before we reached South Carolina we couldn't even speak to each other.

When we got back to Connecticut history repeated itself, as if it were my fate. I was left spending time waiting for him to come home, just as I had been with Keith. When men stop taking you places and they begin to leave you at home and make up some kind of lies; take heed. That's when you know they have replaced you with someone else. I would catch him cheating, but as was my pattern with men I loved; I would forgive him as if nothing happened.

A NEW HIGH

From there I got introduced to cocaine by my coworkers. I learned to snort the white powder and loved the way it made me feel. I would only do it here and there. As time went on it became more frequent. At Christmas time our job would give us a bonus check and we would have plenty of money to spend on cocaine. I loved coke because it made me work faster. I was attracted to its strength and the ease in which it worked in me.

My coworkers began to talk and shared accusations that Johnny, my brother, was shooting up drugs. I didn't believe it because I thought he was scared to stick himself. He would be scared to get a shot at the doctor. I knew he was doing cocaine, but not heroin. One day we purchased cocaine powder. He took his and went in my mother's house with it. A man was outside fixing my car for me. I tried to go inside to do some cocaine and my brother had the chain on the door so I couldn't get in. I got angry and kept ringing the doorbell. I later found out that people on drugs don't like noise. He had no choice but to hop to the door with his pants down, which exposed the needle in his leg. That's when I knew for sure that he was shooting up. Since then, he didn't hide it from me.

BROTHER'S TRANSPLANT

My brother's kidneys started to fail. He was going for dialysis three times a week. He would be so weak when he came home and my mom couldn't stand it. She wouldn't leave the doctor alone. My brother needed a kidney transplant and I knew it had to be me. They had to put me in the hospital for three days of testing to make sure it was a match. One of the days after the test, my brother and Devon came and snuck me out of the hospital to go to Main and Tower and get drinks. After a couple of hours they brought me back to the hospital drunk and I put my night gown back on. After the third day, I went home. They told me that I was a perfect match for my brother, but I had too many main arteries so it would endanger my life to do the process. Only if he was about to die would they go through with the process. My brother was still drinking and doing drugs. The doctors were aware of this and didn't want to take my kidneys and shorten my life. Why should they when my brother was going to destroy his own life regardless? They figured it was better to take a kidney from someone who had already passed away. My mother would call the doctor three or four times a day until he got a kidney from somewhere. She was not going to sit idle and let her son die. At least not on her watch...

One day I was getting ready to leave for work and the phone rang. It was the doctor's office saying they had a kidney coming from Florida and my brother only had a couple hours to get there or else they would give the kidney away. He was usually always at the house, but for some reason this day we couldn't find him. We rode up and down the streets and had neighbors and friends outside looking for him. When I got back to our street the neighbors told me he was on his way to the hospital; my dad was taking him. My mom was in Alabama on vacation when the call came for him to get a kidney. She had to find a way to be there during the surgery. As soon as she could she took a plane from Dothan, Alabama to Atlanta. There she could catch a plane to Bradley. She was scared because the plane was shaky, but she had to get back for her son. She made it in time for my brother to get his transplant. I was so happy that he had a match that I went to the florist and got him a big bouquet of flowers. Just as I got to the hospital room a nurse stopped me and told me I couldn't bring the flowers in. All that money I spent on the flowers was a waste when I could've used that for drugs. Yes, that was my mentality while using cocaine. The kidney transplant was successful but it didn't stop my brother from doing drugs. Not by a long shot!

HELLO? IT'S ME, KEITH...

One random day Keith had called me on the phone to apologize for messing up my life. Two hours later he was admitted at Cedar Crest Hospital. This was a mental hospital. When he was there he had cut his wrist. I felt sorry for him, but I was not taking him back. I was through! I still loved him, but I knew I had to love him from distance. It was for my best interest and safety.

Sometimes we fall in love with someone, but the other person is not in it. With Keith and I, our goals were not the same. My goal of being a mother and house wife did not match with Keith's goals of living the fast life. When you're not going in the same direction as your lover it's difficult to maintain because there's no balance. You cannot make someone love you.

DRINKS AND ENGAGEMENT

After my arguments with Devon I would meet him at Main and Tower. I knew he would be there because we hung out there a lot. I would walk into the bar and he would come over and order drinks for us. He would order shots of Hennessey and light fire to it. The key was to drink it while the fire was still burning. He would order more and I would drink more. This cycle would continue throughout the night until he found out that I was crazy enough to keep drinking. Only then did he stop ordering drinks.

I thought Devon had been cheating because he wouldn't come home on Fridays. He would be drunk and out riding around with women. I was about to put him out of my apartment but he suddenly asked me to go to Bill Savit's. It was there that he purchased my engagement ring. I was so happy! I was not looking at the fact that he was an alcoholic. My sincere love for him overshadowed any negative thoughts I had about him.

I had been snorting cocaine casually, but I didn't need it. It was just for fun. One day I was at my cousin's house with my brother. They knew I had cocaine because they saw me snorting it. They asked me to put mine with theirs so they could cook and smoke it. I inhaled it and I didn't like it all. So, I transitioned back to snorting it versus inhaling it.

KEITH SHOT

I've had so many hurts in my life. One day a friend of the family called me and asked if that was Keith who was shot at an after hour party. They heard about it on the radio. I went to the hospital to see if it was true. I did not know what to expect. I didn't even know if it was my ex-husband or not. When I got there his girlfriend tried to stop me from seeing him. I lied and told the hospital that he was my husband because even though we were divorced we still had the same last name. They allowed me to see him. His intestines were hanging out and he was unresponsive. My ex-husband was shot three times with a 357 magnum gun. I thought there was no way possible that he was going to survive. Remember, at the age of 15 years old he had been shot, stabbed, and left for dead. I went back to my mom's house where I was holding a large insurance policy on him. I thought he was going to die this time so I repaid the policy. God was not ready to call him home at this time either. He lived to see another day.

THE HANDS OF TIME CONFRONT KEITH

Two years later, on a hot summer day, my aunt was visiting from Alabama. She and I walked into a shoe store. I saw a pair of shoes that caught my attention. I looked at my aunt and told her,

"These are a beautiful pair of shoes to wear to a funeral."

I remember telling her,

"If I should die today, life doesn't owe me anything."

My aunt looked at me and asked why I said that. I honestly had no idea why I did. An hour later, after dropping her off, I received a phone call saying that my ex-husband had been found hanging in his apartment. This was so hard for me. I was in shock and my soul was devastated. Even though we were not together we still regularly talked on the phone. My son was only ten years old at the time of his father's death. Even though my husband was not spending a lot of time with our son, my son still knew a little of his father. Financially I was already a single parent, but at this point I was really going to be a single parent. Reality began to kick in harsh and fast.

I was able to go to the apartment where Keith hung himself. I went with his mother. I found a journal that he had written. It detailed that he was going to commit suicide and where as well. I also saw things about his childhood in this journal. I stood in the exact spot where he did it. I stood there and stared at the ceiling amazed. There were questions about murder, but I knew it wasn't murder. His house would have been torn up if some-one tried to kill him. I was in shock the whole time I was there. It was a lot to think about. Even though he hung himself I still considered him to be strong. I think it takes a strong man to hang himself. I just couldn't believe his life had gotten that bad that he couldn't take it anymore. He must have had a lot of broken pieces. It was sad that the choices he made in his life had taken him to that point. His girlfriend had walked in and saw him hanging. Frantically she attempted to save him by cutting the rope. The neighbors said that Keith had told them that he was going away. They told him to stay in touch and Keith responded by saying,

"There is no writing where I am going."

Keith usually spoke with a hard edge so the neighbors never thought anything of his words.

I would wake up in the middle of the night and cry nonstop. Devon just couldn't understand the fact that we were sleeping together every night, yet I was crying over another man. That man happened to be my ex-husband and my first everything. He didn't know what it felt like to lose an ex-lover to death. He could never understand the purity and sincerity I had for him. Perhaps no one ever could...

MY FIRST CONDO

I purchased a town house condominium that Devon and I moved into when I was 30 years old. Devon never paid anything. Just after moving in I had an alarm system installed. The alarm company told me for every new customer I gave them they would give me one hundred dollars. I saw dollar signs because there were 52 condominiums there. I walked to every condominium and tried to sell the product. On the way back to my house I ran into Devon and his friend. He asked me to loan his friend one hundred dollars. I told him that his friend didn't have a job and I then asked how he was going to pay me back. Devon said if his friend didn't pay me back then he would. I knew he wasn't going to, but I gave in and gave him the one hundred dollars having not the slightest idea of what they were going to do with the money.

When we got to house we sat upstairs in my den and they pulled out the drugs. They began to smoke crack and passed it to me. I thought it would be just like snorting cocaine, but I was wrong. From the first time I pulled it I fell in love. I gave them another one hundred dollars. When it was all gone I remember sitting on the floor and begging for more. This was one of the lowest days of my life. I was hooked from that point on. Every day that I came home from work, my hunger kicked in, and I would give someone money to purchase crack for me.

I was caught in an ugly cycle and did not know how to find my way out. Satan is clever and smart. He is always a step ahead of you if you don't know how to get away from his traps.

Chapter 7

BUYING DRUGS

In the beginning I was afraid to go buy drugs because I did not want anyone to know that I was using. I would always give someone the money to go and buy them. They would always tell me they lost the money, got beat or that it wasn't real. I later would find out that they kept the real drugs and switched them with sugar, sheet rock, or anything that looked like drugs. I got tired of people using me for my money. I would complain to my brother about getting ripped off. My brother tried to persuade me not to smoke it, but he realized I was already hooked. He told me that if I was going to use it then I had to buy it on my own. I was out of my league and I was now in a new ball game. One day when I was getting high and my brother said,

"If only your mother could see you now, what would she do or say?"

I was the one that was supposed to do something with my life. Now I figured if I was a machine operator for the rest of my life that would be okay because it was a good paying job. I began to buy my own drugs, but sometimes I would still buy imitation drugs because I would not take the time to look at it. I was afraid the police were going to come or someone would see me and tell my parents.

At first I would stay up late at night getting high. Then I would have to search every coat pocket, pants pockets, purse; you name it. I searched everywhere I could think of to find some more money. I had to vacuum the floor with my hands. I carefully picked up everything that looked white in prayerful hope that it was a rock of crack cocaine. I even looked on the floor of rooms that I had never been in. I had to find a way to get the money and it became harder and harder. Once I got the first hit I had to get a second one. The craving had a stronghold over my mind and body. Captain Cocaine was going to get in my head and tell me how to get more. At this point it didn't matter even if I chose to steal from my parents. It did not matter how big or small the lie was. As long as the lie got me more cocaine I was going to utilize it. It got to the point where I could no longer get credit from my drug dealer because my bill had gotten so big. This is how strong the addiction really was.

This would go on for about 19 years. I could not even work a full 8 hours because my drug was calling me. I really did not have a choice when Captain Cocaine called me. I was going to find a way to make him happen, even for a minute, to get him off my back and out of my mind. I would try to say not today. I would even break the pipe but I would either have to run to the store to get another pipe or wait to use someone else's pipe. I would even try to find a soda can and put holes in the top. I did not like the can because I would always lose too much of the drug. I loved the nip bottle because I could control it better. At first I was afraid of the glass pipe because you were not going to lose anything. Soon enough, all I wanted was the glass pipe. My mind submitted to it and it knew it.

Devon started working at a produce place downtown and they would pay him cash every morning. My brother and I would be at his job right when he got off at about 8 a.m. every morning. We did this so we would have money to get high all together. This lasted about two months until he couldn't stay up and work all night anymore.

HANDS OFF OF MY SON

One day when Devon was so drunk that he passed out. When he woke up he said something to Keith Jr. and Keith Jr. went into a fighting stance. Keith Jr. wasn't a little boy anymore and wanted to prove that. I told

Keith Jr. to come with me to the store. Just as we got back Devon came out of the house like a crazy man. He was irate and furious! He grabbed my son by the chest in full attack mode. I started hitting him in defense of my son. A police officer was across the street and witnessed the entire event. One thing that would always sober me up was if Keith Jr. needed me. The police knew me because we used to work together. He grabbed Devon and threw him in the car. He was going to arrest him, but I told him not to. Once again I chose to save the abuser. I was always looking out for someone else's feelings only for them to come back and use me.

I went to my parent's house and asked them for money to pay for a bus ticket to send Devon back to South Carolina. This was his hometown. I had money, but I had to save it for drugs. My mother didn't trust either one of us at that point so she went with us to the bus station or we sent him off. She stayed there until he got on the bus and it pulled off. This was the official confirmation she needed for her peace of mind.

FROM CONDOMINIUM TO BASE HOUSE

From then, my addiction took off again. I continued to chase drugs. My condominium turned into a base house. Everyone would come there to get high. Most of the time my son was at my mother's house. However, when he was home I would make him stay upstairs.

My brother would hang at my house and do drugs too. One night he went into a violent seizure. The house was full of people getting high and smoke was everywhere. My brother had his kidney transplant about a couple years before. My brother came over to me and told me that his heart was hurting. I yelled at everyone to get out and I had to call the ambulance. No one moved! My brother started having a bad seizure right in front of my eyes. I called my parents and told them that the EMT's and I were taking June to the hospital. When we got in the ambulance he turned into the

Incredible Hulk. He was trying to bite the EMTs. The EMTs were trying to hold him down, but didn't want to get bit. God allowed me to hold him down even with a cast on my arm. I had surgery performed on it from being a machine operator. Finally, by me holding him down, they were able to drive to the hospital. When we got there they ran all kinds of tests on him and asked a bunch of questions. He told them that he had been smoking crack. The doctors came out and said,

"He'll be fine as long as he doesn't smoke any more drugs."

I got very offensive and said,

"He wasn't doing any drugs."

They told me to sit down because he already had told them the truth. They probably knew I was on drugs too because my eyes were most likely popped out of my head. My parents took us home from the hospital. My brother went home with them and I went back to my house and continued to get high. There was so much smoke you could barely see. This was becoming the norm in my condominium now base house. I adapted to its environment because I allowed my addiction to create it.

Three months after that I went to have surgery on my other hand. I left my car with my brother so that he could bring me and pick me up. But, when I called him to pick me up he didn't come. I had no choice but to call my mom. By then I had gotten extremely sick and was throwing up. The result was that I had to stay another night at the hospital because of this.

When my brother came to get me my car had a big dent in it. I asked him what happened and he said he didn't know. I later realized that he didn't know because he was having black outs. The next day I was late paying my car payment. If I didn't pay the bill it was going to get repossessed. My brother told me he didn't care and went in the house to lie down. God gave me strength to drive to the bank to get money to pay it. A week later my brother was driving my car and hit something else. It just seemed destined for him to have bad luck with my car.

My arm was hurting so bad from surgery. I kept trying to call on call to get in touch with the doctor to ask what he could do to assist me. While I'm calling I watched my brother popping an abundance of Ibuprofen pills. He said his head was in excessive pain. Over the course of an hour he had taken around ten pills. I didn't think he would overdose because of his tolerance from all the drugs he had taken over the years. He looked at me and said,

"I wonder what would happen to you if I wasn't here to protect you."

It was as if he felt like he was going to die. The look in his eyes was darkened like black clouds. They were drifting away from this Earth slowly but surely. He pleaded with to stop going back to Devon. He knew that I had a history of taking back men that hurt me and he didn't want to see that anymore. He then laid his head back on the pillow and fell sound asleep.

NO MORE PAIN, NO MORE SUFFERING... R.I.P.

A couple weeks after that my mom got up one morning to get dressed for work. She went into the bathroom and saw blood everywhere. She went in my brother's room and asked him if he messed up the bathroom. He said,

"No ma'm."

But she knew he did because it was only three of them in the house. He lived with them his entire life. She knew he must have been very sick. She went to get my father and had him call the ambulance. My mom called me and I immediately went to the hospital. That afternoon we went home because he was settled in his own room. When we got to my parent's house I was laying on the couch thinking,

"Good, I get to lay on the couch now."

Since my brother had always slept on the couch. Something told me I should get up and clean my house because June might not be coming back. I didn't know why I thought that but I didn't go home. I stayed there and proceeded to clean.

About three that morning the house phone rang. It was the hospital requesting us to come as soon as possible. When we got there June was in the intensive care unit. The head doctor came out and told us that he was brain dead. He was hooked up to a life support machine. Even though they said he was brain dead from the beginning, they continued to leave him hooked up to the machine for five days. We watched them administer medication to him and it gave my mom hope that he was still alive. She would just lay there, rub his head and tell him how much she loved him. But, the entire time he was dead.

The very first day at the hospital I remembered that my friend Carol worked there. I asked around about her and when I found her I told her what was going on. Every morning when she got to work she came to my brother's room to check on us. We never left the hospital. On the third day there we were just sitting in the room and my mother talked about the chain my brother had. My brother would pawn this chain every month. He would go back and get it on the third of the month when he got his check. I remembered the last time he went. He told me to pawn it; so it was in my name. I don't know why he told me to pawn it, but it was like the Holy Spirit stepped in. June knew he wouldn't be able to go back and get it. I abruptly left the hospital and went to the pawn shop. I purchased the chain and brought it to my mom. I told her I knew June would want her to have it and I presented it to her. Her heart was filled with joy. I could tell because although her voice was speechless, her tears spoke volumes for her.

My dad decided to go back to work to get his mind off of what was going on. The next day I called my dad at work and told him to come to the hospital. I knew my brother was going because his body was starting to smell. We called the hospital minister to the room and he released my brother back to God. The nephrologist was called and he took my brother off of life support. Carol came around as usual and she came at the moment when the doctor was disconnecting the life support machine. They warned us that my brother's eyes may open with the disconnection and they did. His body also began to swell. Then, it was all over. Carol cried and I had to hug and hold her in my arms. Supporting her took the focus off of me crying. Carol and my parent's exited the room back to back. We thought my mom was going to tear the hospital a part, but she walked out like a champ. I felt like no one cared about me. June was my only sibling and he was now gone. I had to drive myself home with no one to support me. I remember driving around for a while and eventually I did what I always did; I found a score and got high.

A couple of times that night I felt my mom come and rub my head. She would talk to me as if I was her son instead of her daughter. Johnny was her world! Sometimes I honestly believed that she wished it was me instead of him that died; even though she loved both of us unconditionally.

We planned to have Johnny's wake here in Hartford and then fly him to Alabama to be buried. At the wake I began to shout and speak in tongues. It was the Holy Spirit, but my father believed it was the drugs. I stopped the whole wake because everyone began looking at me. Someone had heard that if one sibling died then the other would die soon after. My parents didn't know what was going on with me. My girlfriend Vickie remembered that the church she belonged to was having choir rehearsal next door. She ran to get someone who worked in the medical field to come assess me. The ambulance came and took me to the hospital. Sadly, the wake was over...

After they got the medication from the doctor I got released from the hospital. The medication was meant to calm me down. The doctor knew we were going to a funeral in Alabama. My parents, son, and I got ready to go to Alabama to bury June. We buried him and left him in Alabama. One day after my mom retired her plan was to move back to Alabama. Her wish was granted.

WHY DIDN'T YOU TELL ME?

We didn't know my brother had aids until the funeral home. The funeral director pulled out the death certificate and asked if we wanted it to be passed around. I don't know how God allowed my eyes to go straight to the line that read he had aids. Before my parents could answer I took the paper and said,

"No, we're okay."

After we left the funeral I told my parents what the death certificate said. My mother was already hurting because he was a kidney transplant patient and he had just died from having a tumor on the brain. She now was forced to add this to her list of agony with her son and deal with the fact that he had aids. She completely freaked out and called the doctor. The doctor informed her that he couldn't reveal this vital information because of patient confidentiality. My mom was looking at me like, "*Why didn't you tell me?*" I told her that I never knew. No one ever talked about it again. It was laid to rest with him that very heartbreaking day.

We go around and sleep with men and women because of how they look on the outside. However, we never know what is on the inside of them; physically and spiritually. I never knew my brother had AIDS, in spite of being an IV user. I would have loved him the same anyway. I wanted to talk about it but I couldn't. My family was kind of the quiet type. I told my Aunt Chris, Uncle Jim and that was it. My Aunt couldn't understand why my mom didn't tell her. I had no answer for her and didn't try to offer one. Only my mom knew why she didn't tell her. I didn't talk about it any longer for a couple years after that.

My drug problem had gotten much worse. I couldn't work anymore because I had too many surgeries on my hands from the 13 years of doing repetitive work at the factory. I got on worker's compensation, which gave me full access to getting high all day and all night. I would always wake up my son no matter what time it was. I'd ask him for money nonstop. He would tell me no, but my request persisted. If I knew he had money, even a couple dollars, I would annoyingly ask, ask, and ask until he finally gave in to me. During the few times he chose not to give it to me, he knew I would eventually start searching his room.

I would occasionally see Sean from time to time. It seemed liked yesterday when I was sneaking him in my apartment, which took place years ago. It might have been months or years later, but he always seemed to reappear; even without me calling. I decided that I had to get a job because I was so accustomed to working and I also was desperately trying to break the cycle. I was searching for a way to get off of drugs. I acknowledged that idle time in my mind had me imprisoned as a child on Satan's playground.

FIRST 10-DAY TREATMENT

My son took me to treatment for my drug addiction. He came to my girlfriend Betty's house because I was there all day getting high and drinking. I was trying to go out with a bang, a grand finale; because I knew I was going to treatment. I called my mother and told her that I needed a couple of more dollars. I had to explain to her that they wouldn't enlist me in to treatment unless I was really high. I had to get to treatment by a certain time and was grateful that Keith Jr. picked me up and took me to Reed treatment. I did really well there. It was a 10-day program. My parents came to bring me something and were asked if there was a history of alcohol or drugs in the family. My mother said no, but my dad said yes. Both of my dad's parents were alcoholics. As a child I remember witnessing my grandma being passed out on the porch from alcohol. Her husband died from being intoxicated, as he crashed into a tree drunk driving.

I knew I had a desire to be like my first drug and alcohol counselor. I admired her and I loved the way God used her to touch his people's lives. I also loved her red sports car. I really thought I was cured when I graduated the program. I felt completely different and had a confidence in myself that was absent for years. Yet, I wondered how I would deal with temptation once I wasn't in the 4 walls of the Reed Treatment center.

My son came to pick me up from Reed Treatment. When I got home I sat on the front porch because I knew my room was a mess and I wasn't ready to go see it. I finally got up, walked in the house and proceeded to my bedroom. I walked in and it was spotless! My son cleaned up everything. He didn't want me to come home and find anything related to drugs. He did a beautiful job and it truly helped me make it through that day.

Something kept telling me to throw my mom's key down the drain so that I wouldn't go in her house to get money to do drugs. I knew if I saw ten dollars then I would take it and go buy drugs. The next day I needed gas money so I went to my mom's house. There was a note written from my mom, to me, on the table. I was supposed to be looking for a job. I took the note and it read, "*I hope you use the ten dollars for the right thing. I love you.*" With no hesitation I went to buy drugs and then directly to my girlfriend's house to get high. I felt so bad because I had just gotten out of treatment and betrayed my mother's trust with no hesitation.

My son moved out and into his girlfriend's house at about age 17. He began to sell drugs and sold enough to purchase a car. One morning he left school early to make a drug transaction. He was rushing to get back to school and he hit a light pole that fell on top of the car. He crawled out of the car through the windshield with his leg dangling. No one could explain how he did it because as soon as he got out of the car it caught on fire and burnt all the way down to the frame. His girlfriend's brother happened to be driving by and saw the accident. He called his sister and she in turn called my mom. She then called my dad and they all went to the hospital and stayed with him. I just happened to call my father and he asked where I was. He told me that Keith had got into a horrific car accident. Sadly, they weren't even going to call me because they figured I had a job and preferred that I stay at work while they supported my son. As I was going to the hospital unknowingly I drove by the scene of my son's accident. The workers were fixing a light pole. I was fussing about what fool hit the pole and eventually came to find out that it was my son. I got to the hospital right before he went into surgery. It was a successful surgery and he was fine after that.

Chapter 8

A NEW MAN APPEARS - MICHAEL

I met a guy named Michael during the first day of my new part time job. I was working as a security guard. His friend looked out the window and told him there was a pretty new lady working at the front desk. He peaked through the window and he liked what he saw. He made a ten dollar bet with his friend that he was going to get me to be his girlfriend. Later when he took his break he made his way over to me. He began to talk to me about drugs and alcohol. It was as if he was in my head. How was he able to read me so well? I now know it was because he could tell by looking at me that I was a drug user.

I found out how he knew so much because he had lived in the drug world. He had been clean for about a year when I met him. This time I was in for the ride of my life. When I first met Michael I was not in love with him. It really did not matter if he came by or not. I had lived a very busy life at this point. My time was consumed by trying to smoke crack cocaine and having fun with a couple of other lovers. By this time I was just going to play the field. I was free and I was never going to allow another man to get close enough to my heart to hurt me. No one was going to have my heart again!

After I allowed him to finally come to my house, we began to spend more and more time together. We became lovers after a week of him coming to visit. We would spend every minute together and there was never a dull moment with him. Eventually we both fell in love with each other. He would always encourage me and I loved that about him. I would sneak and get high before he came to visit. I would always know the time he was coming because he was married. In the beginning he always went to work at night. I was back and forth from his house too, while his wife was at work. All she had to do was come home to catch us. It was risky but the thrill of it was adventurous and a turn on.

In Michael's eyes I outshined most of the women that he was accustomed to being with. One main reason was because I owned my own home. I had to live a double life by living in the drug world and maintaining a beautiful house. Awkward as it seemed it did have a unique balance, which I maintained.

Michael would pay close attention to every word I spoke. I wasn't used to people paying attention to me with sincerity like he did. He would look me in the eyes and repeat every conversation we had. He had a way of making me feel so important that you would think I was the only woman in his life. He specialized in knowing how to treat me when I was with him. He would study me and tell me not just what I wanted but also what I needed to hear. He also knew how to hold a woman the way she wanted to be held. He brought a peaceful security to my life at the time and when we were together we shined.

I never felt like the other woman with the men I dated. It was as if the wife was the other woman. It was always exciting when he would come over. There were no limits to him and me, so it seemed. Michael would always tell his wife some lie to get out of the house. He would tell her that he was with his boys. Therefore, I never had to spend the holidays alone. He would spend a couple hours with her and the remainder of the time with me. Was this sinful? Yes… but it was a balance of love that I cherished with all of my heart.

OUR BOND STRENGTHENED

Around the fourth month of us being together we sat in the living room talking one day. Michael said to me,

"Brenda you are pregnant."

I said, "No way."

I went to the store and brought home a pregnancy test. Surely, I was pregnant. Michael told me that I could not keep the baby because he was married, still living with his wife and because I was still using drugs. We both agreed that I would have an abortion.

A couple of months after the abortion we started living together. His wife couldn't take our love affair anymore. We were so good for each other and he became my drug. I would go to AA/NA meetings with him just because he was going. I was able to stay clean for one year without a program, because of his unwavering and consistent support. I didn't realize that I wasn't using drugs until one day my father approached me and told me that he was so proud of me. I asked why and he said because I was not using drugs anymore. I was so shocked and honestly didn't realize it. All of my focus was on Michael and I was grateful. This was a gift from God! The next time I picked up a drug it would not be so easy to get off. About a year later I was pregnant again. Michael and I were really happy. However, two months later we found out that I had a miscarriage.

My counselor would always tell me that my mom was my enabler. I would get so angry and tell her that she had no idea what she was saying. I began to tell her that I was grown, had a son of my own and had a good job. What I really wanted to tell her was that she was jealous because her mother could not afford to do the same for her. I did not ask for her opinion and just needed her to take me to the meetings. I was in such denial. I would say to myself, "*You don't even have a job; at least I work every day.*" It would be years before I realized that she was right. Let the truth be told: I did not realize until this book was almost completed. That's when I honestly admitted it to myself. Deep down in my heart I knew my mom was doing a lot for me. I knew I could not stand without her help. I knew my mom would not help me pay my bills if I didn't do what she said.

CAREER MOVE

Michael began to bring out the best in me. He would motivate me to do different things. The more he encouraged me, the more I would do. I began to attend Morse Business School in Hartford. Michael would always come by after school and we would spend hours together before he went to karate practice. After karate practice he would return for another visit. He worked at night so he would always leave my house before going to work.

Michael was also always there every step of the way to help with my school work. He was even there for my graduation from Morse Business School. That was my first graduation. I attended this business school for one year and received a certificate. The one thing I liked about Michael was that he never wanted to hide me. He always wanted to show me off. I got my first business job too, through a temp agency, but I didn't like it. The only part I did enjoy was the expectation of getting dressed up every day. I loved dressing up and looking nice, but I knew I wasn't going to make it in the business world.

RELAPSE

Michael met someone in the AA program and began spending a lot of time with her. I asked him why weren't we spending time together anymore and he couldn't handle it. He was getting pulled in too many directions and sadly he relapsed.

I went shopping downtown to get my mind off of him being with another girl. Shopping was my first drug; it was called retail therapy. I arrive at my home and my son and his friend are sitting on the front porch. My son would come over sometimes to check on me. He told me that Michael had been looking for me. I walked in the house and there he was sitting in the bathroom with the pipe in his hands. I didn't even think twice. I joined him and told him to give me some. We then ran in and out of the house the entire night looking for drugs. I was hooked on drugs once again. We began to call the drug dealer after the banks closed. We gave the bankbook to the dealer and we were able to get drugs throughout the night until he would not answer the door or the phone. He would come in the morning to take us to the bank to get the money. Every day was the same thing until there was no money. I loved Michael; make no mistake about it. However, please know that the spirit of influence is very real and powerful. I joined in with him willingly; by loyalty but more so influence.

ATTEMPTING TO GET CLEAN

I tried going to a detox program three different times. The detoxes lasted about three to five days each. I would stay there and attend the groups they held. They also created a treatment plan for you. They encouraged you to not go back and hang with the same people who were negative influences concerning your addiction. It was basically a place to go and get the drugs out of your system. But, once I was away from the facility I would go right back to hanging out with the same people and doing the same drugs all over again.

I went to ADRC Treatment for three days. This was another detox. I ended up leaving to go get high with Michael. I simply could not shake my addiction. My brother-in-law brought me to UCONN hospital. It was located in Farmington, Connecticut. However, when we arrived there were no rooms available. Michael and I walked all the way from Farmington to Hartford. It seemed like it took us forever to reach home, especially since we had no food and were both coming down from a high. We lucked up and found an apple on the way home and shared it. Our bond was very strong.

TRYING OUTPATIENT TREATMENT

I checked myself into outpatient treatment because I knew I needed to make a sincere effort to deal with my addiction. Once there I met a counselor that captured my interest. I don't quite how I started talking to him but one day he met with me and we rode around in my car. He was very encouraging and positive in supporting my efforts to get assistance. I loved the way he compassionately spoke to me with such calmness and care. He paid so much attention to detail in everything I said. I had developed a strong liking for him. Truthfully, I had a crush on him.

Michael was very familiar with everyone in the program because he was in and out of it himself. One day Michael was outside working on his car. I walked over and began asking him questions about this counselor. The more questions I asked, the more agitated he grew. Michael must have caught on that I liked this counselor by my nervous mannerisms while asking him questions. His eyes squinted and his deepened as he said,

"What you like him or something?"

I gently responded,

"No, he's just my counselor."

Michael gave me a look of death and slowly nodded at me. His eyes were set ablaze with an anger that I was all too familiar with. One day he wasn't home for the entire day. I had the counselor's number so I called him a couple of times that day. My son still had his own phone line in his room, even though he had moved out. I kept the phone in there because I would still use it from time to time. The counselor didn't answer any of the times that I called, but he ended up calling later that night. Michael heard the phone ringing and sat up with a confused look on his face. He violently said,

"Keith don't live here anymore! So why is that phone ringing?"

I was so nervous that I couldn't speak and I sure didn't dare to go and answer the telephone. Michael picked up the phone and asked,

"Who is this?"

The counselor said his name and title. Michael slammed the phone so hard that it almost broke. He swung and punched me directly in my face. I tried to cover up but it didn't work. He continuously punched me in the face until it was bloody and swollen. He became the next man in line whom I loved and got beaten on by.

Michael saw the counselor in the street a few days after. He honked the horn and pulled over. I was so embarrassed that I wanted to hide. Michael rolled our car window down and told him to never in his life talk to his woman again. The warning was issued and heard loud and clear.

BACK AT IT LIKE IT NEVER LEFT

When there was no money available to purchase drugs we began to sell my clothes and household items, such as stereo systems, to get money. We both had the best of everything. At times we would have three of our cars going up and down the street. We had rented them out to the drug dealer in exchange for drugs. We even bought groceries and ended up returning them to the store to get our money back to spend on drugs. This was so embarrassing for my son to see and experience his mother while she was heavily on drugs. He had to listen to his friends call his mother a base head. But, he never stopped loving me. My son told my father that he did not hate me; he just didn't like the things that I was doing.

If I borrowed a dollar from my son, he would come to my house and wake me up to ask for his dollar back. Even though he didn't live with me anymore he used my home to hide the drugs that he was selling. I would search the entire house looking for money or drugs. I didn't care which one I found, but if it was drugs that would be easier. When I was high I would get so paranoid to the point where I would get scared of my own shadow. At that time I was using a nip bottle to smoke out of. I would run to my son's old room and throw the nip bottles out of the window. They were piling up on the lawn quickly. The neighbor told Michael that he would see me throwing them out. Michael came home and said,

"If you don't go clean those up, I'll…"

I went outside and it blew my mind to see how many nip bottles were in the backyard just lying there. I picked them all up and Michael and I got the residue out of them. Then we went inside and smoked the leftovers.

One day Michael and I walked in the house after going out to buy drugs. I had left the curling iron plugged in. I looked on the floor and the curling iron had caught on fire. I could not put the pipe down to put out the fire. Michael said,

"Fool, don't you see the rug burning?"

And he put it out for me. I was too absorbed with the pipe to even have a live fire catch my attention. This was the power my addiction had over me.

One day I was really high. Michael picked me up and told me he was going to bring me to my mom's house. I told him I was not going to my mom's house. I was not going to allow her to see me that filthy. I was in the passenger seat and I reached over and put my foot on the brake. A car hit us and I told them to keep going.

MICHAEL'S WRATH

My relationship with Michael became very abusive. Michael would get high and become very jealous. He would accuse me of being with other guys and always accused me of stealing drugs from him. I finally got tired of his behavior and I knew I had to get away from him. I feared for my life. Once he got so angry with me that he threw a knife at me and it landed in the kitchen cabinet just above my head. Michael and I were always breaking up and getting back together. After each break up I would always show up at a meeting that I knew he was going to attend. In my heart I was not ready to give up on our relationship. I truly loved the way he made me feel, outside of his physical abuse. I finally realized that Michael did not trust me because he was such a woman's man. He loved women and most of his relationships came from women in the program.

Michael asked me to marry him more than once. I just knew that it was never going to work. I think if my mother was not in the picture then I would have married Michael a long time ago. My mom knew we were not good for each other. The only thing Michael and I had going on at this point was good sex. This was the one time that we could connect and forget about our problems. This was another thing that we had in common; lust. I had learned how to satisfy my man instead of doing school work, for example.

MY PURPOSE

The Holy Spirit directed me to my purpose in 1992. This was done while I was visiting my mother-in-law in the convalescent home. As I watched the CNA's come in and care for her, I noticed that they had such a grace about them. I admired the way they handled her and moved around. Through them The Holy Spirit showed me my next assignment: to go to school and become a CNA.

I immediately started doing research on how to become a CNA and within a couple months I applied to Greater Hartford Community College. I had been on unemployment and they gave me money to go to school. I got into the program and it was only about 11 weeks. I really wanted this to work, so I actually studied in the midst of getting high. In order to complete my course I had to do an internship. I was very good at it until I found out that I had to clean poop. One day on the internship a patient had pooped. The instructor told my colleagues and me that we had to clean it up. I thought to myself, "*Not me! I didn't even clean up my own baby's poop. Keith Sr. used to clean it.*" I ran to the bathroom until I thought they were done cleaning. It wasn't easy going to school because I got high every day after school. However, I shined through because the love I gave to the patients was genuine.

I completed the internship with such grace. This was the one time I really felt that I could love these patients and touch lives. I've always had a caring heart and wanted to help people, but I always got abused by the wrong people. I finished and received my CNA certificate. I didn't realize that cleaning poop was actually a big part of the job. I had no problem getting my first CNA job and it was full time. Even with the blessing of a full time job I was still getting high. If the monkey got on my back while I was at work I would tell my job that I had car problems and had to leave. Then I would go get high and go back to work the next day. If I didn't go to see my mom then she would call the job and ask where I was. She was hoping in her heart that I wasn't getting high, although she knew I was.

My mother would continue to leave me notes of encouragement, especially if for some reason she had to leave money. She hoped that I would do the right thing even though she knew in her heart that I would not. I kept the letters she wrote to me forever.

1. Brenda we love you so much, so live for us. You can do what you want to do. We want you to do good. You don't have to do bad. We did not bring you up like that. You can be that good Brenda if you want to or keep doing what you are doing. You will be dead where your brother is; you have a choice good or bad.
2. Brenda this is all I have. You can take 10 and bring me back 10. Love ma. Be good and good luck.
3. Doing drugs is bad. We don't want you like this. We want to be proud of you again so make up your mind. Love you, Ma.

My mom would dial my number and call me back to back. I would just sit there and look at the phone ring. I knew if I sounded high she would come over. My father used to tell me to pick up the phone and say 'I'm okay' and then hang up; just so they knew I was okay. But, I couldn't do that because I was too scared she would be knocking at my door if she felt that I wasn't okay.

TWO YEARS LATER
NO MORE MICHAEL

One time too many, Michael and I had been getting high all night. We were smoking up the mortgage money. Michael promised he would help get the money back. The next day I asked Michael for money after he got his check and he told me no. That was the straw that broke the camel's back. I changed the locks and asked Michael to leave.

Later that night my mom called my girlfriend's house. She told me to go home because she had received a call saying that my condominium and my car were on fire. Michael was on my girlfriend's other phone line. He was out of breath and asking me what I was doing. I immediately hung up with Michael and went to my house. When I got there I saw that my car had burned to the frame and the side of the condo was melted. To this day, although it was never proven, I believe in my heart it was Michael who burned my house and car. I went into hiding at that point. More than ever I feared for my life at the hands of this man.

I knew that I was finished with Michael, especially when I stopped going to places where I knew he would be, such as the AA/NA meetings. It was easy for me to stop going to these meetings because most of the time I was going with him or just to see if he was there. I didn't go anyplace where I knew he might be. The only place he knew to look for me was at my mother's house. By this time I walked away from my house because I had realized I couldn't afford the condo while getting high at the same time. I was always falling behind with the mortgage too. I had to work extra hours or ask my mom to help me.

MOVE TO EAST HARTFORD

I realized I was too hooked on drugs and I had to get away to start fresh. My son and I moved from Hartford to East Hartford in my late 30's. I figured if I got out of Hartford and that house then I would be able to stay clean. I was able to stay clean for about two weeks after the move. Then, I was using drugs as if I had never stopped. I was there for a year using drugs heavily, but I always made sure to pay the rent.

About a year later I lost my job for no call, no shows. I would be too high to go to work. I would stay up too late and I was always getting high. I was terrible in every way possible and truthfully I just didn't care.

My girlfriend Sharon came over one day to cook breakfast for me. I wouldn't eat when I got high and I was very skinny. Sharon loved to feed me and she also had a crush on my son. I was so tired and had been strung out for two consecutive days. I was a smooth talker and could talk circles around Keith Jr. Keith Jr. told me,

"You keep talking... Mama is on her way."

The house was a complete, dirty mess. I took the table cloth and threw it out with everything in the trash. The rest of the house was still a mess. My mom and the police were the only ones I really feared. Keith had told me a little too fast. I told Sharon,

"Let's go, right now!"

And I left before my mom could get there.

I started boosting to get money. I would go to the store every day for about two months and steal a lot of items. I didn't fool with any cheap stores at all. They had to be expensive stores. A girl from one of the nursing homes I worked at taught me how to boost. We would come out of the stores and compare who got the most stuff. I realized if she got in trouble, then so would I. So, I started doing it myself and it worked better that way.

After we stole the items we knew someone who would return them and get 50% cash credit. That way we would get more cash. Late at night if I had merchandise lying around, I would sell a three hundred dollar outfit for five dollars; just to get high.

SUGAR DADDY PLAYED SWEET MUSIC IN MY EARS

One day I was leaving my house to get cigarettes. A white guy about twice my age yelled to me from his car. I was not interested, but for some reason I gave him my number. He told me that his name was Joe. He called me the next day. I ended up going to his house and slept with him in order to get high. This continued every day or night that I wasn't working. He would take me to Hartford to get drugs. He liked the excitement of helping and watching me get high. He never did drugs, but he did drink beer. I just wanted to use him for his money and I honestly had no feelings for him whatsoever. If there was days that I didn't want to be bothered I would still have him bring me to Hartford. When we got back to his house, before he parked the car, I would take off running. He felt used and would come to my house and blow his car horn like crazy. It didn't matter what time of night it was, he was desperate to find me. All of the neighbors knew that he was coming to see me. One day I told my girlfriend's daughter where I was going to be. She told my son because they had grown up together. I used to deny it to my son, but he knew about it and would tell me to stop.

INPATIENT TREATMENT

Everyone was sick of me; from my son, my mom, to everybody. I had been running and running and I had to go to treatment to show them that I could do something right. I knew to call Blue Hills Hospital and asked if they had a bed. They told me yes and instructed me on when to be there. I told them I couldn't go that day, but I could go the next day. That day I had to go out with a bang and get super high.

I went to inpatient for 30 days at Blue Hills Hospital. I packed all my pretty little clothes and short skirts. I was wearing a short dress and go-go boots when I got there. I wore clothes like this all the time because I knew I looked good. I walked down the hall and the monitor said,

"You need to go change your clothes."

I said, "What do you mean I have to change? I came here for help with drugs, not my clothes!"

I got so mad I called my parents and said,

"They're telling me what to wear!"

My parents came running because they didn't want me to leave. The residential monitor began to talk to me and told me to stay. He also took time to talk to my parents as well. I said,

"I'm going to give this mess one more try..."

The case manager came on Monday and pulled me in the office. She said I couldn't behave like that. I was humble and said I was going to make it. I began to like it there and even actively participated in the groups. They had meetings all day long so I went to all of the meetings. They had outside people come in and I would say that I was going to stay clean. I had the talk down to a science and really believed that I was going to get off drugs.

I had to listen to the voice of the Holy Spirit. I not only had to listen, but follow His direction. This was not always easy because in the world of sin I did not follow anyone's directions. I just did as I pleased, even when I knew there were consequences to my actions.

When I was in treatment I was always able to hear God's voice. While in treatment the Holy Spirit came to me in a vision and told me that I was going to be a minister. Again, I believed it, but had no idea how He would make that happen. I only knew one verse from the Bible and that was John 3:16:

"For God so loved the world that he gave his only begotten son…"

My mom knew at this point that I would sell everything for drugs. My mom had bought me an expensive bracelet in hopes that I was clean. One day it came up in group discussion that I no longer had the bracelet. My parents were there visiting and my mom directly asked me where my bracelet was. Everyone began looking at me. I didn't want to answer her at all. It was the hardest thing for me to do in telling my mother that I sold the bracelet for ten dollars worth of drugs. I was honest like my counselor had taught me to be. My mom asked who I sold it to; as if she was going to try and get it back. My dad brought her back down to reality and told her to let it go.

We had a fashion show one night in the treatment center. I had my girlfriend bring me a black suit. I had a nice shape back then and this suit helped show it. I went and sat down next to the guy I liked. His name was Randy. I had a thing for light skinned men. An outside girl had said something very rude to me because she was jealous. I could tell she didn't like me and probably liked Randy too. I knew I couldn't say anything back to her because I was the one getting treatment. I went to the monitor to tell them to get her away from me to avoid trouble. They acted on my request and the girl got loud with them. Since she caused a disturbance they asked her to leave. It was easy too because she was an outsider. I was supposed to get called in the office to talk about this guy three days before graduation. I packed up my stuff and called my girlfriend Gloria to pick me up. I left there thinking I could stay clean. I figured those three days weren't going to make a difference. I didn't have enough sobrieties under my belt to stay clean, so I went back to what I knew; the drugs. Randy and I still found time to talk and exchanged numbers. He called me to his house the next night and we got high.

Randy knew I used to steal because we had to talk and share out in group sessions. He figured since we were out of treatment that I was going to go back to stealing. Randy asked me to steal watches and I said that was not a problem. I stole three watches in one day. I got caught with one, but I was so scared that I gave the store detector two of them. I still managed to keep one. I want you to know that even in my mess my God watched over me.

My life was becoming unmanageable again so I went back to Blue Hills Hospital and they let me do the detox again. The staff told me that I shouldn't have messed with that boy. I left again after the detox. I had enough of the program. I realized that I was not finished running after my drugs. I would run all day and catch the stores before they closed to steal things so I could support my habit. Randy would drive my mom's car because I was too tired to drive. I let him take the car and he ended up taking it for three days. My dad came to my house early one morning and went into the hood and disabled the engine. I wasn't able to leave with the car after that. My dad showed me that he was getting tired of my messy lifestyle.

I got another CNA job at an assisted living facility. I was still using, but I was able to hold it down. One night I left my money in my locker at work. I left it there purposely to stop me from using it to by drugs. But, I ran out of drugs and returned to my job to get the money. I was high so I hit the wrong numbers for the key code. When I tried to open the door the alarm went off. Everyone came out looking. I was high as a kite and the coworkers stood there staring. My supervisor watched me when I came to work because she did not want me coming to work high. She knew I was getting high out of work, but she would always say, *"If you're worth the fight, rules can be broken."*

I was eligible for medical insurance on my ninetieth day of work. It was a Saturday and my supervisor came in. If I got on medical I would be able to go to treatment for free. She asked me if I was using drugs and I told her yes. I cried and cried and she sympathized with me. She told me to go home and try to get in to treatment.

6 MONTH TREATMENT

I found Blue Ridge Treatment Center and told her about it. She told me to stay in touch. They did an assessment on me and my case manager told me right away that thirty days wasn't going to be enough for me. I had to go somewhere for a longer period of time with my history of drugs. I cried my eyes out because I wanted to be drug free, but I didn't want treatment. I told them I had a house and I didn't want to go. It was a hard decision to make, but I finally surrendered because I had thirty days of sobriety under my belt and thought I could keep going. They found a six-month program for me. They gave me four hours to go home and pack an entire house of furniture to put in storage. My mom helped me put my stuff there because I couldn't afford to pay housing rent if I wasn't going to be living there.

I was placed in Clayton House. You had to work and have your own bank account in order to live there. They let you go to work and have your own transportation. I was lucky enough to have my own car.

Everyone had a day to cook. There were men and women living on the facility. All the case managers said I was the most stubborn person that they had ever met. Before God delivered me from drugs, He had to deliver me from Michael. Please understand that Michael was a dangerous drug for me. Even though I wasn't with Michael, I would still run into him at the meetings. The case managers and clients put me in the middle of a circle to try and get me out of denial. They would try to get me to see from different points of view. I would get so angry and cry. I would turn the entire house upside down. I would leave meetings and stomp up the stairs. They didn't know what I was going to do. They would have to stop the meetings because I was making so much noise over their head.

They also tried to get me to stop shopping because they knew that was my first addiction. One day my housemate asked me to take him shopping. I wasn't going to just take him and not buy anything for myself. But, when we got back to the facility he told on me in the meeting. I said,

"You were the one who asked me to go."

I couldn't believe he told on me after he asked me to go. They reinforced to me that I couldn't go shopping anymore. I learned not to trust him anymore after that situation.

I really enjoyed being clean and free for those seven months. That was the longest that I had been clean in a while. I learned a lot about myself there, such as how to get through the grieving process of my brother. They would tell me to get in a comfortable spot and they would play music with the lights off and talk to me. I had to allow myself to enter into a special place in my mind. After I went through the hurt I had to write a letter and then go outside and burn the letter. This was teaching me how to release pains once and for all.

Every Sunday we had to go to an outside meeting at the YMCA in East Hartford. Right after the meeting my church would come in and have mass. I would stay for church services and I would shout. I would watch Bishop Barbara shout. I thought it was so beautiful to see Co-Pastor pregnant and still praising God. I asked God to give me that praise and dance because I could feel the power in it. Some of the girls in treatment with me would stay at church with me and watch me praise God. Then they would do it themselves. Then we would talk about it in the meetings. I always praised God from a little girl, but I hadn't done it like that in a long time. There was power in my shouting and in my praise!

I was grateful for AA and NA. I loved hearing people share what they have been through. The speakers who were in recovery would speak and I would always tell them I was grateful for them being there. It seemed like they had more sobriety. I looked at my counselors and God was speaking to me in spirit that I wanted to be a drug and alcohol counselor one day. I took heed to His words and meditated on them day and night.

When I graduated they put me in a circle and I got to invite whoever I wanted. I invited my counselor from Blue Ridge because she played a big role in motivating me to stay clean. Everyone got in a circle and said something positive about me. Even though it wasn't easy I had made it and gave all glory to God. It was a big accomplishment, especially since every-one didn't get to graduate. I thank God for allowing me to make it. It was a big stepping stone because I didn't finish anything back then.

I was happy to go out and live by myself again. I felt a new sense of freedom. The day I got out I moved into a new apartment in East Hartford. Unfortunately, the spirit of chasing drugs was waiting for me, not as a neighbor but as my roommate. I was also still working at the assisted living facility as well.

I was blessed to have the opportunity to pray for sick patients. There was one guy that we knew was dying. We were in the middle of serving lunch and I had told Rose I had to go to Bill's room. The other staff person was mad, but let me go anyhow. I cleaned Bill up and gave him his last rights. Bill opened his eyes after three days and said,

"Thank God." I left the room and my supervisor walked in the room right after to pronounce Bill dead.

AFTER TREATMENT

The next year my mom removed her name from the lease. I remained in East Hartford for another year and had some home care jobs. I was back to getting high and being paranoid once again. I always feared the cops would catch me with something in my hand and arrest me, so I started throwing things. One day I had a lighter in my hand and the air conditioner was blowing. I lit the lighter to take a hit and I threw the lighter. It fell on the dining room table which had a cloth on it. I quickly ran out of the room. When I got back, the whole table was on fire. And this was a very expensive Pennsylvania house table. I put the fire out and left the house.

I used to hate driving back from Hartford. I would be so high trying to drive that I would pull over on the street and look around to see if the cops were coming for me. I used to pray to God during the drive to get me home safely. Even in my sin I called upon the name of Lord and He truly kept me safe. I say that to encourage anyone reading this book who feels abandoned by God because you may be trapped in sin. He is the only one who can save you. Seek His face daily and establish a relationship with Him. I lie to you not; He is a faithful and just God. He is a rewarder of those who seek Him diligently. I'm living proof of His glory.

One day I had gone to Joe's house to get some money. He was fussing at me like always. He gave me the money and I left to go to Hartford. When I came back a state trooper was parked on the other side of the street. I didn't see him right away because he was blended in with the other cars. When I got out of my car I saw him standing outside of his car with his foot on the bumper. I knew he was waiting for me, but I was not paranoid because I was not high. I walked up the long walkway and felt the officer's presence behind me. When I walked left to turn into Joe's house, the cop turned right to see me fully. Something told me not to go in the house to get high. I had hid the drugs in my mouth. I faked ringing the doorbell and acted like he wasn't there to answer. I went back to my car. The cop said out loud,

"She made me."

If I had went inside I would have been smoking the cane and I would have been so bugged out. When I got high I used to spray the entire house and then run and lay on the couch. A bad side effect of the drug was paranoia and I would act sleep because of it. All of my neighbors knew my routine and that I was doing drugs. We were in and out all night long and Joe didn't have any shades. They knew I was tricking to get high based off of these patterns.

The cop had been there wanting to bust us. A couple days before that one of the neighbor's friends had parked in Joe's parking spot. Joe said he was going to have their car towed and the neighbors wanted to get him back. We knew it was them who had alerted the cops of our drug activity in his house.

SET UP AND SET BACK...

The worst time I had was early one morning when I purchased drugs from an undercover police officer. I was at my house and had been getting high. I was just trying to make it somewhere else to get high. I went to Hartford to the same spot I usually went to buy drugs. There were two guys outside and one asked what I wanted. I didn't answer. They asked again how much I wanted. I had a twenty dollar bill balled up in my hand, but I said 10. They started aggressively grabbing my hands. I thought they were pagers because they were known to try and take your money. I shook myself free and they both said,

"You are under arrest."

They called a police car to come pick me up so they could stay on the block. The police man read me my rights. He asked me what I was trying to buy and gave me a chance to explain myself. I would've said marijuana to get a lesser charge, but I remembered my right to remain silent; so I didn't say anything. He charged me with buying crack and took me to jail.

They booked me in the meadows and threw me in a cell. The police officer that was watching me was my friend. I use to work with her at a grocery store when we were young. She said,

"I didn't know you were back here. I would've talked to my sergeant to get you out."

I didn't dare call my parents to get me because I couldn't tell them I was in jail. I couldn't call Joe because he had surgery. So, I just sat there waiting to get out on my own.

Finally, after a couple of hours the authorities came and loaded those of us who weren't getting bailed out into a paddy wagon. I was very cluster phobic and lost it. I started yelling, screaming, and kicking the doors. When they found out that I was just paranoid they told me I had to get back in there. I wanted them to shut up but I had to hold it together.

They transported us downtown to Washington Street. They put all of us in gender cells and it was so crowded. There were too many women so they had to put two women in a padded cell. I hoped I wouldn't be put there. Instead, they put me in a cell with a pregnant girl. They came around with some tuna fish sandwiches that were soggy from the mayonnaise. I said,

"I don't want that. I want out of here."

The pregnant girl gladly took the extra tuna fish sandwich. Officials started calling names to bring people to Niantic. Then they passed out blankets to people who were not going to make bail. Some people went to sleep like it was nothing. In fear I began acting out by screaming obscenities. The correctional officer said,

"This is your first time, huh?"

"Yes, but I talked to God and told Him if He gets me out of here I'll never do drugs again."

I was then handcuffed and taken to Jennings Road. I was given a PTA (Promise to appear) court date because it was my first time getting arrested.

SERVICE IN MANY WAYS

My car was still on Sigourney Street where I had gotten arrested. I would always get out of the car when buying drugs, because I knew if they caught me buying drugs in the car it would be towed.

From the Meadows is a long walk to get to a main street. It was also late at night when I was released. This random lady was nice enough to pull over with her family. I thanked her and got in. A State Trooper happened to see me and made me get out of the car. He knew I had just got arrested for buying drugs. I was so angry but I made it to the gas station and thankfully a man I didn't know drove me to my car.

I got in my car and went to the ATM to see if I had any money. I forgot that I had money stashed away in my car. Like an idiot, I used that money to go back to the same spot that I had just got arrested at to buy more drugs. I told them to hook me up because I just was released from jail. That's how sick I was! I had just told God I wouldn't do drugs anymore but was right back at it.

When my court date arrived I was assigned 140 community service hours. It was really hard to work full time, get high, and do volunteer work. The volunteers sent me to groups that administered urine test. I was so scared to get tested that I went to Albany Avenue and bought something that would clear my urine. I was so confident, but I flunked it.

When I finished all of my community hours I went back to court. They said,

"One good thing is that you finished your hours, but you flunked your drug test."

I found out that the program I was supposed to be at had no drug tests. I was so upset because I could've been doing drugs the entire time without worrying about it.

Eventually my sugar daddy, Joe, would beg me to stop using drugs. He would tell me that I was too good to continue to abuse drugs. I told him I wanted to go back to Greater Hartford Community College for English. He believed in me and took me to the school. At first he said he wasn't going to pay for it, but he gave in eventually. I only went for about two weeks and then I dropped out. He said he knew that was going to happen. I hung out with Joe for what seemed like a couple of more years.

A good friend that had always admired me before I was on drugs came and took me out of the base house one day. She told me to stop hanging at that base house. A couple of days later she and I went to the store and returned to the cops surrounding the house. I used to tell the base heads that I didn't want to get in trouble and they would tell me that I wouldn't. They all ended up getting arrested that day and God revealed to me that once again it was He who saved me.

I WAS USED AS A VESSEL

As God prepared to break me down, in order to build me up, He stripped everyone from me to clear the way. On my way to work one morning something told me to call Joe. It had been a while since I last talked to him. He answered the phone and told me he needed medicine because he was really sick. He didn't have anyone to get it for him. I called out of work that day. I went to Joe's and he was just lying there helplessly. He asked me to go to the bank with his debit card to withdraw money. I withdrew four hundred dollars from his account for myself and I also used his credit card to buy the medicine he needed. I stayed and cared for him for three days. I told him,

"You know that you're dying, right? Do you accept Jesus Christ as your Lord and Savior?"

"Yes, yes I do."

The very next day Joe died. God used me while I was high to help Joe give his life to Him. God truly used me as a vessel of His.

BLOOMFIELD

My son purchased a house in Bloomfield in 2000. He wanted me to come live with him so that I would be away from the drugs. The night that we were supposed to be moving in I was home getting high. He kept calling and asking me where I was. I ended up leaving the house because I was so high. He didn't give up and came looking for me. He strongly desired for us to move in together at the same time.

When I moved my mom came to the house and asked me why we didn't have a dining room table; specifically the Pennsylvania house table. I couldn't tell her that I had lit it on fire. I was too embarrassed and made up a lame lie that I don't think she believed, but didn't question either.

I continued to purchase and use drugs from Hartford. I messed up my son's house from getting high every day. In a paranoid state I would take bleach and throw it on the carpet because I thought the police were coming. I would also spray his cologne until the bottle was almost empty to cover up the smell of the cocaine. He would ask me if I was touching his cologne and I would say no. I also used to go in his room and steal his watches for drug money. I pawned them at the pawn shop. He would ask me if I saw his watches and I would say no. He knew I was lying because whenever I got my check I would go back and buy the watches. They would magically reappear back on his dresser.

He finally put a lock on his door that I tried to pick to no avail. Out of frustration I started throwing my pipes behind my dresser drawer. Once I wanted a hit I would go back and move the dresser. I would be thrilled to find them because they still had cane in them.

On an average day at 2 p.m. the neighbors knew it was my time to get high and a show was getting ready to start. I would always put blankets on the windows because cocaine makes you paranoid. The more I smoked the more paranoid I would become. In fear of going to jail I would take a hit and take off running downstairs and hop in Keith's bed before he put a lock on his door. I would pretend I was asleep in case the cops came looking for me.

I would drive around in broad day light and at night smoking crack cocaine. I thank God for covering me and pedestrians because I never hit anyone with my car. He covered me during a time that I was standing in the bathroom smoking crack. My arm had caught on fire and I could not put the pipe down to put the fire out. My arm was burning like a piece of meat but the power of the pipe was my only priority. Until I got my full hit the fire would have to wait. Yes, I was a real life addict; under the submission of cocaine.

I didn't even have money to buy medicine for my arm. It was a hot summer and I had to wear long sleeves to cover up my wound. The next day at work I showed my coworker, Rose, this gruesome sight. She had compassion on me and purchased me cocoa butter and medicine. God allowed me to have no scars on my arm; none! I was so thankful for my coworker. Understand that God places angels in your life for certain seasons.

My mom never wanted me to be without money. She would tell me to drive from Bloomfield to her house in Hartford to get a few dollars. I made that work because I would get my drugs while I was in Hartford. I didn't have gas to drive there from East Hartford after church. I would make sure that I got my drugs before going to church. I would always stay for the entire service because it would be so good. I am sure there were times that I would take the drugs, along with the cigarettes, in the church.

I would go to the cleaners and put all of my clothes on separate tickets. This particular morning I went to the cleaners before I got high. I wanted to get some of my clothes out for church that Sunday. I had to go early morning so nobody would see me. I put all my clothes on different tickets because I didn't have money to pay for them all of them at once. I had the lady pick out some of my outfits to choose from. I heard a voice behind me.

"Give this lady all of her clothes. I'll pay for it."

I was so blown away. He told me that he loved Jesus and was a member of First Cathedral Church. He told me to select the best outfit and wear it to church that Sunday. God had placed angels all around me more than I knew. This man knew there was something inside of me. That something would turn out to be the almighty God!

Chapter 9

MY TURNING POINT

One hot summer day something told me I had to cook a family dinner. I was asking my mom to help me. My mom said,

"You're crazy! You don't have money to buy all that food."

But, as usual she helped me. Something told me that would be the last time I was going to get her to help me cook.

One day I went to bring my dad food. I was high but something kept bugging me to go. When I got there he said that my mom was sick. I was baffled because I was just talking to her and she was gardening. I walked in and saw how sick she was. She was throwing up a lot. I realized it was going to be hard to get her into the car to take her to the hospital. I asked my mom if she could call the ambulance and she said yes. That's when I knew her physical condition was severe. We got her to the hospital and they called in a gastroenterologist doctor to look at her. My mom was diagnosed with colon cancer. The cancer was moving swiftly throughout her body. She had to have surgery right away and they said she would have only had two hours to live if she hadn't come to the hospital. God used me to save her life. After the surgery the Holy Spirit revealed to me that I would only have my mom for two more years.

I found out from the many surgeries performed on my hands that I was able to be retrained. They said I could go to trade school, but preferred college. They had me come down to the office and test me. They told me I couldn't go to college because I wasn't college material. I hate when people tell me no and it only fueled my drive to prove them wrong. The Holy Spirit spoke to me and told me that He was sending me to college. I was a person that had a hard time my entire life in school. I always believed in God sending me to college, even though I didn't know how or when it was going to happen.

I told my mom that I was going to college and she said,

"If you don't sit your dumb butt down… You don't even know your times tables."

Aunt Chris was the only one in my family who went to college. My mom began to see me going, but I didn't finish anything. So in her eyes she didn't believe I was going to finish.

Chapter 10

COLLEGE

I could not write a sentence when I began college. I went to MCC. I used to sit at the table in English class and try to write a sentence. I couldn't write sober, so I definitely couldn't when I was high. Karen used to help me over the phone from South Carolina. This went on for a long period of time. I began to try myself after the second year. I was still calling Karen, just less. My father would tease me and tell me to call Gloria for help. He knew that she didn't know any more than I did because we played hooky together every day in high school. He would laugh about it because he saw how I was struggling trying to learn. I didn't know which form of 'there' to use. But I was going to do this if it was the last thing I did because God was directing me. I used to tell the teachers "You're going to help me" and I used to go for tutoring. The retraining people saw me trying and said "You are so determined". They paid for two years of college for me. I was so grateful. But I was still getting high. I would go home after school and get high, then go take care of my mom and spend the night with her in the hospital. I did this every day.

A WORK BEING DONE IN ME

I worked for every treatment center that I had been in. My first job in the field of drug and alcohol counseling was at the Alcohol and Drug Recovery Center. I had applied and got hired on the spot. This was the best experience because it taught me everything that I know today in this field. I could work all three shifts by myself if I had to. There were one hundred and forty co-ed clients. I ran a group for new clients and it was so powerful. A lot of old clients even asked to be a part of it because they enjoyed it so much. It was mandatory that these clients went to church. They would see me praise God and they began to shout, cry, and praise God as well. My pastor at Agape and the members of the church would pick up clients and transport them to church on Sunday morning. The turnover rate for the clients was very high, yet multiple clients would tell me that I was the one who got them into church and for that they were grateful.

I was working part time at ADRC so I started looking for full time jobs in the newspaper. The Holy Spirit told me that the Salvation Army would be my next job. By this time I was smoking two packs of cigarettes a day. I was a heavy smoker. I would try to stop on my own. I would break the cigarettes up and throw them in the trash. Eventually I would go back and get them because I just could not stop smoking them.

As the Holy Spirit revealed, I started working at the Salvation Army. I would bring my clients to church in my dirty beat up Infiniti. I would wear my church hats and dress nice no matter what. My clients were grateful that I brought them to church. The Salvation Army had a trip to Hershey, PA every year with the clients. Vans would come in from everywhere. I was asked if I wanted to chaperone and I told them I didn't want to go. They pleaded and asked me to think about it.

The Holy Spirit revealed to me he was going to help me, but I had to go on this trip to Hershey, PA. I told God I would go if He did two things for me.

1. Stop smoking
2. Tell me when I would leave this job.

I decided to go on the trip after all. The closer to Hershey we got, the cheaper the cigarettes became. Everyone kept telling me to buy them, but I said no. As soon as we stepped out of the van in Hersey, PA I never smoked another cigarette again.

That night, as a group, we went to church. A man was giving a testimony of how he used to be on drugs. He spoke on how a woman invited him to church, but all he wanted was money. She said she would give him ten dollars if he went to church with her. He ended up going to church and becoming a member. I felt all of the Holy Spirit at that moment and I started praising God l fervently in front of the big audience. I didn't care about everyone laughing because I understood the power of my praise.

When we got back to the hotel a female lieutenant came over to me and said,

"There she is! There she is!"

You are the lady who was shouting and praising God at church. She began to minister to me and tell me about the power in my praise. She saw something special in me. She gave me her name and number and me to call her at any time. Tears rolled down my eyes and God told me that I couldn't leave the Salvation Army just yet. I still had to touch more people's lives.

To this day people come up to me in stores and on the street to tell me they are alive because of me. One specific woman kept relapsing, but told me I helped her follow her dream of becoming a drug and alcohol counselor. You could never put a price of watching people grow to be a spouse and have kids because I helped them. Yet, please know that I am boasting about me. No, I am boasting on the grace and mercy that God has given me throughout my life. I tell them to praise God and give Him the glory, honor and praise. It's not about me; it's all about God!

Professor Bobby Fox was my Professor for the drug and alcohol class. I flunked a class and she had to tell me that I flunked and was going to be kicked out of the program. I cried and the more I cried, the angrier I got. I said,

"You think you've seen the last of me, but I'll be back next semester!"

I held my word and went back the next semester. She would write on my papers that I was ready to be a drug and alcohol counselor. She wouldn't write this unless she meant it. She watched me grow and I was ready to be a counselor. After it was all said and done, she approved me and watched me blossom into a beautiful flower.

Bobby Fox's main saying was, *"You can't ask anyone to do anything that you are not willing to do yourself."* It's easy to tell people what they should and shouldn't be doing, but we have to be able to do it first. Bobby Fox uses me today as an example in her class. She tells my story to the students who are struggling so that they can make it if they don't give up. To God be the glory!

Pastor Don Johnson was put on this earth to touch the broken-hearted. He went to college and took the same drug and alcohol class as me. He was so anointed and God allowed me to draw from him. He had the spirit on him and I had the spirit on me. We just so happened to do the same class and internship to reach out to people. He didn't know how much strength I was drawing from him. I didn't know how to walk into an internship, but God showed me how to get there. Pastor Don began to draw people from the Salvation Army to his church and he reached them. They didn't have money to put in for offering, but they were there for God. He attracted many addicts to him. Together we would touch the clients and they wanted what we had. The internship was at my job, the Salvation Army. I was able to get paid and do an internship at the same time.

God replaced all the drug addicts with ministers. God allowed me to walk strong and I began to touch other addicts because I didn't hide anything. I had the real life experience of having walked in their shoes. I would be in the store and people would come up to me and say,

"You don't remember me, but you touched my life."

That is something money can't buy.

I began to church hop because I was shouting in my short skirts and I didn't want people to know that I wasn't yet fully delivered. Agape Church moved from the YMCA to East Hartford. Because I was in the middle of my addiction, you could not count on me. Every time I walked into Agape, Pastor Taylor would always say,

"Good morning, sister Brenda. How are you today?"

I was not used to anyone calling me sister because on the street my name was base head. Every time the prayer line was open, I was there. I knew I could not waste any time. I knew I was going to jail or going to die; I didn't want to experience either one of those.

DEAR MOMMA

I knew that my mom had been my enabler although it wasn't intentional in a negative way. It's a painful thing to sit back and watch your child, someone that you carried inside of you for nine months, do wrong. Being a mom myself I truly can identify with her. A mother only wants the best for her child. When your child is hurting, you hurt. My mom was always caring for my brother and me. My mother was so hurt when she found out that she not only had one child on drugs, but two. I was the one that went to work every day; the one she could always call on and depend on. I was the one that loved to stay home a lot at one point. I was the one that loved to make a home for her son and the one who was going to make her happy by any means necessary.

My mother had been through chemotherapy, but it wasn't working. The cancer had returned and the only other option to slow it down was to have a hysterectomy. She had to go back to the hospital but was not ready to die. She didn't want to leave us and would do anything that would prolong her death, even if it was only for one day. She was willing to go through it for her family.

My mother loved me so much. Lying on her death bed but she was still willing to give me life. My mom knew I had no blood pressure pills and as well as no way of getting any. I was not at the hospital when the nurse came in and gave her blood pressure pills. She took the pill out of her mouth and put it underneath her pillow until I came. There were other visitors in the room so she called me over to her side and whispered in my ear,

"I have a pill underneath my pillow; take it."

"No way...You have to take your own pill."

The Holy Spirit showed me that she was being sent home to die. The doctors in the hospital said there was no more that they could do for her. They knew she was very close to death, but they didn't know how many days she had left. The Holy Spirit told me that she was going to die on that Thursday. My Uncle Jim was here from Alabama and he was the only one who believed me. He left on that Wednesday because he didn't want to watch her die. He told me that he was not worried about me because he knew at that point I was counting fully on God for help. My Aunt Chris was about to leave, but I told her to look at my mom. My mom had wanted her to stay. I was thankful that my Aunt Chris was there to help and take some of the burden off of me. I was still trusting God through it all. All I had was faith in Him.

My mom would ask me to tell Pastor Taylor to come and pray for her. Then she began to ask a little too much. I would call and ask him if I could put the phone to her ear and would he pray for her. He told me no, that he would prefer to come to her. When my pastor got there, I asked,

"Can you please take my tithes to the church?"

I gave 10% of every pay check to the church and began to give to the church regularly. I wanted the church to be able to pray for the next broken soul that came through the door.

That Thursday morning, on March 18th 2004, Pastor Nash of Mount Cavalry Church came to visit my mom's house to pray for her. My father said that Pastor Nash prayed so hard that my mom's eyes opened after being closed for two consecutive days. When he arrived I took it as my cue to go get high. In my mind, no one was going to miss me anyway. I forgot it was Thursday because that was usually my day to go get high. Everywhere I went to get high no one wanted me there, even though I had money. I had money because I was writing myself checks from my parents' bank account. I thought to myself, '*I'll just go back to my mother's house.*'

As soon as I walked in, the Holy Spirit spoke to me and told me this is the day I am taking her. God had answered my prayers by not to be letting me get high that day. God was showing me His faithfulness over my life yet again. My brother had died at the age of 33 years old from drugs. It was not enough to stop me. God spoke to me loud and clear. God made a covenant with me that day. He told me to tell my mother that it was okay for her to die because He had me covered. I was able to tell her because I believed it. He told me that He was never going to let me fall. His words were, "*Will you trust me?*" and I said "*Yes!*" I told my mom that the Holy Spirit had told me to tell her this. She believed it and she was able to let me go and let God have His way. To this day God has kept His promise. I have never been without Him; God had always been with me. Though I walk through the valley of death, I thank God for being my savior. I cried unto the Lord and He heard my voice. Grace and mercy shall carry me through all the days of my life.

SLEEP IN PEACE QUEEN

I entered my mom's room by myself. I looked at my mother and knew this was it. I called the hospice nurse and I told them that she was getting ready to die. I asked if I could give her more morphine. The nurse wanted to know what type of work that I did. I told her that I was a Certified Nursing Assistant, but my work experience had nothing to do with me knowing that she was dying at that moment. I was listening to the voice of the Holy Spirit. The nurse said no, but I was persistent until she believed me. The Holy Spirit confirmed that my mom was dying within an hour.

I got into the bed with my mom. I laid my head on her shoulder and was able to tell her how sorry and how thankful I was. I'm grateful to have been able to release her to God. I thanked her for giving me life and loving me; even though I was a drug addict. I began to repent for the disappointment that I had caused her. I told her that God was waiting for her and that He had just spoken to me. He told me,

"I got you. I will never let you fall." I believed Him. As soon as I told her that God spoke again and said,

"It's time…"

I never thought twice and reached for the Bible. I read one line to her with her in my arms. She took a deep breath. I looked at her and read one more line. She then took her last breath. God honored my dream to have my mother in my arms when she passed. I am grateful that He did.

I was sold out to God. From that point on He had kept His promise. I was the only one in the room with her when she took her last breath. I believe she was able to die in peace because God assured her that He had me. My mom had been trying to hold on because she did not know what was going to happen to me. I was a believer from then on and listened to God whenever He told me to do something.

As soon as the Washington's heard about my mom's passing, they were on the scene. As soon as Donna found out my mother that she had passed away, she began looking for a way to Connecticut. There were no trains or a bus going out fast enough; only a plane. Who else do you know that would take a plane from Rochester, New York to Hartford, CT other than Donna Washington, to be with a friend? She knew I was about to lose my mind without even telling her. She's a true friend for life. Vickie was there within minutes, along with my cousins Mary and Mable. Mable's son Marquis came too.

My cousin Mable and her son Marquis came to my mother's house to console my family. As soon as they returned home they found her husband, my first cousin, in the chair dead. Their funerals were a day apart in Alabama. The funeral people said that they had never had this happen because the same people that were at my mother's house, were now at his house.

PASSING ONE TORCH TO ANOTHER TORCH

My church choir sang at my mom's eulogy. It was as if it was not a wake. I just gave God all the praise and danced before Him. I was able to fly to Alabama with my family, bury my mom, and get back on the plane to get home in time to walk into my final exams. God told me I would be drug free one year before I graduated college. I was more determined than ever because God had spoken it. But most of all, I had faith that it was going to happen. It was not easy, but with the help of my family, friends, church family and God; I made it. My son had also asked my father to move in with us so that he wouldn't be alone in Hartford.

God began to do new work in me. I cried before the Lord and He heard my cry. I told him that I wanted to stop using drugs. This wasn't the first time, but this time was different. I did not want to become a fifty cent whore. I would go on the front porch early in the morning and began to read my bible. I would read it before and after I got high. I began to church hop again because I did not want anyone to see me shout and cry more than twice. I did not want people to laugh and talk about me in church, because I had enough of that happening in the streets already. I just wanted to be healed and delivered from drugs.

We never know the effect we have on people when they walk through church doors. Pastor Taylor at Agape would always ask Coretha,

"How is sister Brenda?"

It was always sister, no matter if it was weeks or months since the last time he saw me. God then spoke to me and told me to join Agape Fellow Ministries and be covered by Pastor Eugene Taylor. My son would come into my room on Sunday and ask,

"Mom. Why are you not getting ready for church?"

I would tell him that I had no gas in my car. My son would give me two dollars. He didn't care how I got there, just as long as I got there. I had been in and out of Agape and I began to make deals with God. I asked him,

"Why are you putting me at a church so far away? There are churches I can walk to and my car has over 300,000 miles on it."

"Do you trust me?"

"Yes, I do trust You Lord."

A week later my car went down. A week after that, I had a brand new Infiniti paid that was paid for in cash. That's just the way God works.

I was always testifying in church of how I could not stop using drugs; how I could not hold my money without spending it on drugs. I would always have to ask other people to hold my money. I had to tell on myself to be set free. I had to humble myself and have humility. I had to realize that everything I had tried to do on my own was not working. I had to listen to the voice of the Holy Spirit. If He told me to turn right, I had to turn right. If He told me to turn left, I had to turn left. Friends and people that knew I was using drugs began to call me a hypocrite. I never looked at it as being a hypocrite. I called it desperation and also knew I was making steps to be whole in Christ.

I wanted to pay my tithes, but I told them I used it on drugs the night before. I couldn't hold it. Minister Hughes told me,

"If it is your desire to pay your tithes then I can help you. I'll come to any base house and meet you. I'll take the money and ask you no questions."

That blew me away. When I got my check I would call her and she would tell me where she was so I could bring her money before I got high.

My son began to see a change in my life when I began to go to church regularly. Sister Cheryl would bring me handkerchiefs to church every Sunday, because I was going through so many Kleenex tissues. I would cry so much because God was cleaning me out. I believed my deliverance was in my praise because the Holy Spirit spoke it to me. God, I thank You for favoring me. Who would have ever thought that I would get to know You the way I do? Everyone around me was saying,

"Irene is gone now. What is Brenda going to do now?"

Everyone that knew me saw that I was sinking deep in sin. Everyone around me had given upon me. I broke every one of the 10 commandments. The drugs had become my God that I would worship day and night. The Lord said that He is a jealous God.

A BLESSING IS BORN

My son, Keith Jr., had a baby boy and named him Anthony. My first grandbaby was born in December of 2005. He would come over on the weekends when he wasn't with his mother. He was about six weeks old and I was babysitting him. I wanted to get high so I drove to Hartford. I left him in the car and got the drugs. I got home and got high with no hesitation. I told myself, *"I can't babysit this baby high."* Soon after, that was it! It was 2006 and I was sober from then on. God convicted me that day and freed me completely from using drugs. My grandson, Anthony, was used as the vessel. I give God all the glory, honor and praise!

GRADUATION

Minister Hughes came all the way from Utica, New York and sat in that hot sun to support me. She showed her big smile and embraced me with a hug. My dad was smiling from ear to ear. My son looked at me and said,

"You did it! Mom, you did it!"

I invited my supervisor and clients that were in the Salvation Army and they got to witness what God did for me. My supervisor said she wasn't coming, but she was there with a big bouquet of flowers. I was so happy! It was the happiest day of my life. It wasn't just about the associate's degree. Instead, it was about what God did for me, for His glory. It was evident that God had done just what He said He would do. I now know that God allowed me to attend college and equipped me with an associate degree. This was the key that was going to open any doors that He needed me to walk through and minister to His people. I graduated in 2007; after a year of being clean like God had promised me.

I was like the woman with the issue of blood. I knew that if I just got close enough to God than he would heal me. I believed it and no one could tell me different. I had been praising God consistently, no matter what church I walked in. I praised Him mostly at my house. I talked about His grace and mercy everywhere I went. I was so grateful. I knew that God was going to turn it around in the midnight hour. God had given me a shout. It wasn't a shout of desperation, but a shout of gladness.

CHURCH

There is nothing I loved more than going to church or a place where the Holy Spirit is present. Praising God and being able to have the Holy Spirit on me was powerful. To watch others lift their arms and pick up their feet to give God praise and honor was a Holy Ghost party that I blessed His name for.

When I began to fellowship with Agape Fellowship Church, the only thing I could really relate to was the songs that the choir would sing. It was as if they were singing about my life and how God was going to deliver me. My co-pastor Robin would always say,

"You shall have what you decree. Speak it in the atmosphere."

I would cry the entire service. That was the Holy Spirit cleaning me up from the inside out. I cried for a year. I just could not stop crying no matter how hard I tried. Remember, I had over twenty years of shame, guilt, lust, stealing, and hurting other people. My Heavenly Father loved me unconditionally. The Holy Spirit had to get rid of all those things that had been keeping me in sin. Things that were keeping me from being whom God had called me to be. I would get in the center aisle of the church, close my eyes and cry out before the Lord. The Holy Spirit kept my eyes closed. He knew that I was not ready to see that other members were working on their own mess, just as I was. God knew that if He would have opened my eyes earlier, than I more than likely would not have stayed in church.

When God tells us to pray we have to be obedient and pray. One morning the Holy Spirit had woke me up out of my sleep and had me pray. I don't know what I was praying for, I just prayed and read my word. I thank God for my obedience to the Spirit, because later on I had heard my dad was in a horrific car accident. I know it was because of my prayer that he was able to get out of the car scratch free, in the name and honor of Jesus Christ.

I always wanted to be a blessing to the church even though I could not afford it. I would pick up all the change on the floor and use it to put in the offering. When there was no more quarters and dimes around I had to use pennies. At Agape they told us that if every member of the church gave one thousand dollars for three years, then they would be able to pay off the Church mortgage. The Holy Spirit allowed me to get in line and say,

"I don't have one thousand dollars, but next year I will."

The next year I was able to keep my word. I was able to speak those things as though they were. I thank God that I never had to ask the church to pay anything for me. God sent me to Agape to learn how to take care of myself and to be amongst believers who would pray for me during my battle with drugs. I always had faith that God was going to do it. God wanted to take credit for everything and didn't want me to have to rely on anyone, but Him.

I had watched Bishop Barbara and other members of the church shout as they praised God. I remember asking God to allow me to be able to praise Him too. *Be careful what you pray for because you just might receive it.* I sure did! I have now been praising God for 14 years. When I began to praise God, I would close my eyes and pick up my feet. It was as if I was not here on earth. I would be at peace. I was not about to stop praising God because I had realized there was power in my praise. God's word says,

"Everyone who acknowledges me publicly here on earth, I will also acknowledge before my father in heaven." (New Living Translation - Mathew 10:32)

God kept my eyes closed so that I would not be distracted by things of the world.

I have always said the church was like a hospital. We all know that in a hospital there are all types of sicknesses and illness. People go there to get cured and healed. There are some that will be, and others that will not. I knew that I had all types of health problems going on in my mind, especially having been on crack cocaine for nineteen years. I knew that I could be healed only by having faith. I knew the healing was going to have to come from God. My mom could never understand how someone could holler and shout the way I did. When death came knocking at her door, she then began to understand. Pastor Taylor would always say that praising God was personal because when God comes and calls for you, He will not knock at your neighbor's door.

Every time someone would ask if anyone had a testimony I would never think twice. I was there to tell mine. Members would come to me after service and say,

"Why do you tell your business?"

I would tell them that they did not have a heaven or hell to put me in. They never knew what it took for me to be able to get to church. Never mind getting to church, but the difficulty of just walk into church. The more I showed up to church, the more I was talked about. Coretha would help me get to church. I would sometimes have to drive to her house because I would not have gas money to make it to church. I had to get out of bed and clean myself up after getting high all night.

Some mornings Coretha would have a hard time getting me in church. I remember this particular morning that it was really hard for me to leave Coretha's house. I began to cry, cry, cry… All I could say was,

"I am not going back over there with everyone laughing and talking about me."

Coretha prayed for me. It was as if I would take one step forward and one step back. This was a morning that she had to usher. She was so late, but she would not leave me or tell me to get out of her house. She was very patient with me. I finally explained that I was going, but I was going to sit in the back of the church so no one would notice me. How wrong was I? The church was full and you had to be on time to get a good seat. I didn't know that there was going to be a guest speaker or I would have never gone. I sat in the back of the church and the tears would not stop flowing. The more I tried to stop them, the more they came. I tried to wipe the tears quickly before anyone could see them running down my face. The guest minister was Bishop Roger J. Hairston Sr. He was from Columbus, Ohio. As soon as he was introduced, he began to speak life into me. He said,

"I have a wife at home and I am not trying to flirt. But, this is for the woman sitting in the back with the red blazer on. Whatever your tears are about, it's going to be okay; you are coming out!"

He came down from the altar to my seat. He said,

"This word is for you and after I finish ministering I am going to sing you a song."

I still remember this as though it was yesterday. I can't remember the song or what he preached, but I do know I was touched and it is still with me over 13 years later. I felt that I would not be in anyone's way if I was cleaning the bathrooms at church. I would bring my own cleaning supplies, even though the church had its own. I would clean it as if it was my own bathroom. I have always taken pride in the things I did if I was not using drugs. Members began to make statements to discourage me. I began to think that they believed all I could do was clean the bathroom. I stopped after about a year. I never wanted to be on any committee. I didn't want to get in anyone's way. It was fear that was holding me back. I went there to get clean, sober and to praise God. Every time I would think of doing something I would sit back and watch the members that would come in so strong. Yet, something would happen and they would leave the church for one reason or another. I thought God had me there to bring in people like myself, who were addicted to drugs. I knew I could do that.

Minister Kathy Hughes always prophesied that God was going to fill the church. And miraculously He did just that. They were not people that could pay tithes. Instead, they were broken people who were addicted to drugs, but hungry for the word of God. It is a known fact that most of the crime in our states are caused by substance abusers. While most people are sleeping, the addicts are creeping around in the middle of the night trying to see what they can take to get their next high. Minister Hughes preached a sermon one day that God has to hide you to keep you safe. At that time, God hid me in the church. I thank God that He chose to hide me in the church and not in jail cell.

Herbert Powell once performed a eulogy. He said that an obituary has the date the person was born, a dash, and the date that person died. And then he asked the question,

"What have you done with your dash? And I don't mean dash soap powder."

That statement has been with me for years.

Chapter 11

HOMELESS BUT PROTECTED

I was not thinking about moving out of my son's house because I was comfortable. Even though it was time for me to move, I didn't take into consideration how my living there was affecting my son's life. Getting kicked out was like getting pushed out of the nest by a mother bird, at a time when you're being taught how to fly. I was not trying to fly. I thought I was flying already. I was able to do the things that I wanted with my money because I was only paying a little rent money. Well, I had to be pushed out of the nest in an ugly way.

In 2011 my worst nightmare had come true. I was homeless. I had a disagreement with my son and he put me out of his home. He had been asking me to leave because he had a new wife and she and I were not getting along. My son and his wife changed the lock on the door. I wanted to hit him, but I knew I would have gone to jail. I called the police and I left with tears in my eyes. The police told me I didn't have to leave. But, how could I stay some place where I was no longer wanted? As I began to drive I thought I would spend the night in my car at the truck stop Instead, I came to the church and pulled in the rear. It was dark, but there was a light that came on. I began to read my bible. I read and cried myself to sleep. It was so cold in the car but warm in my spirit.

The next morning as I began to leave I had remembered it was prayer time. I went inside the church and prayed to God. After everyone got off of their knees I had tears in my eyes. I began to speak that I was homeless and that I had just slept in the back of the church. I left the church, went to Dunkin Donuts, and cleaned myself up.

I slept three nights in my car behind my church because I only knew church and work. I would say to myself, "*I wish I had one night to go to a hotel and lay my head on a comfortable bed to get my thoughts together before my next move.*"

But I didn't want to spend money on a hotel because I had to save my money. I didn't know how much it was going to cost me to move. The humility was the reason I could not stay with anyone right away. I would go to Dunkin Donuts every morning to clean myself up. I would take a nap in my car in different shopping center parking lots. I thanked God for the Food Share programs. I always ate their oranges. I loved to go to the ones that would give you a word before they gave the food. They would take care of the spirit man before the internal man. I needed that more than the food because I was so broken down.

God kept me. I had money really saved for the first time, but I was afraid to spend it because I did not know if I was going to need it. I tried to get into a shelter, but they were always full. Strategically I would buy one meal a day. I would sit down on the park bench and talk to God and the homeless people. I gave Him thanks because I had money and a car, but most of all I had Him. I knew being homeless was going to be temporary. I then stayed with my girlfriend Coretha for about three weeks. She would go to work early in the morning. I would get up and leave the house when she did. I did not want to be a burden to her. I would drive to shopping centers and fall asleep in my car. I would only return after she got home.

A FAITH TESTED

I was trying to move back in the apartment that I had before. It had a walk in closet and I figured I could use it to make my bedroom bigger. God said,

"I am trying give you my best and you are trying to put limits on me."

God blessed me with another apartment in East Hartford. My new bedroom was bigger than I could imagine. He gave me the best. I was looking for a job while being unemployed. I accepted this apartment with my last three unemployment checks. I went to my friend Margaret's house to apply for jobs. Margaret was helping me fill out the application for Community Mental Health Affiliates and it was taking a long time because they asked for so much information. I told her,

"Forget it, I'll move on."

That was the enemy trying to keep me away. Margaret said,

"No let's get through it."

They were having a women's fellowship at church. A prophet was brought in to encourage the women. Before closing she looked at me and said,

"This woman is really going through it. Everyone needs to secretly put something in her hands."

Nobody put anything in my hand. Not that I would have taken it, but no one offered. I don't know how she knew, but I was a quarter short of laundry. I learned my lesson; not to depend on anyone but God.

I went to Connecticut Works to look for a job about a week later. I brought in my papers and put them on the table. A lady came to me with her cameraman and said,

"It looks like you've done this before. Are you looking for a job?"

"Yes."

"If you don't find a job, what could be the worst thing that happens to you?"

Tears started flowing as I lifted my head and replied,

"I don't want to be homeless again."

They stopped recording and she took me in her arms. I was showing pieces of a broken woman. God will use anyone to give you a hug when you are at your lowest. I knew she was recording me, but I wasn't paying attention. I was too focused on trying to get a job. Come to find out I was on television. My father told me the next day that he saw me on there. He was cleaning and had heard my voice. He turned around to look at the television and it was me.

I laid in my bed that night praying to God. I asked him to help me find a job. The next day on my way to work I got a call. I pulled over to answer the call, which I usually never did. I would just answer while driving but for some reason I didn't this time. I answered this phone call and it was CMHA scheduling an interview with me. I ended up completing the interview and was offered the position on the spot. I left there that day knowing I had a job, with a start date. They hired me as a Residential Monitor. I was so happy! I said, "*Look at God.*" It was another job that I was able to help people that needed me. Ann, the head supervisor, had given me a chance. I would be forever grateful.

I got my dad an apartment in a senior housing facility in Hartford. I didn't want to bring him in an apartment with me because if God took me first I wanted to make it as easy as possible for him to already be situated. A year from being homeless I was at Saturday morning prayer. God told me to go this particular morning. When I got to church I fell on my knees and cried. God revealed to me that this had marked one year from being homeless in my car. He didn't want anyone to help me because he wanted to take all the credit and get all the glory.

Chapter 12

DADDY

I have always been claustrophobic. I feared being in closed places no matter how large or small the space was. From a little girl my father had been the person that my mom called to get me to take my medication. I remember the medicine being bitter and disgusting. It was because it was castor oil. Anytime my mother felt that I had a cold, the answer was always castor oil. It was a laxative and it would keep you running to the bathroom. It was that thick slimy oily taste. There was always an orange to suck on after the oil. My mother thought the orange made it taste better. The orange just prolonged the feel of the oil going down my throat.

Anytime I was to have any type of MRI or CAT scan my father would always have to go with me. My father had a way about him that said, *"We are not going to make this an all day event."* He would say,

"It is something you need and we are going to do it."

He presented this type of manly authority and he was definitely the decision maker in the family. My mother never took that away from him. She stood in her place and allowed him to be the head to guide his family.

FATHER, DAUGHTER LOVE

I pulled into my father's driveway to bring him to my appointment with me. I stopped to talk to dad's friend that had just left his apartment. We talked for a brief moment and his friend began to explain that my father was not eating. She didn't know what was wrong with him. I didn't think it was of any concern because I was with him three or four days prior. I firmly believe in my heart God will use people as angels. I believe I was really there on this day to serve as my father's angel. I pulled up and blew the horn for my father to come downstairs as always. My father came to the window to tell me that he could not come down. I explained to him that I would be back in an hour because I could not miss my appointment. I knew it could not be too serious because his friend would have told me that something was wrong.

Upon returning, I went upstairs to find out my father was having a difficult time walking. I realized at this point I was not going to be able to get him in the car. I called my son to come help me. Keith Jr. told me to call for an ambulance to come help. Just as we were leaving for the hospital Keith Jr. pulled up. We then followed the ambulance to the hospital. The doctors examined my father and we waited for the test results to come back. As my father sat on the edge of the bed he began to give God glory. He began to tell Keith and me how God had been with him throughout his entire life. He shared how God had opened doors in his life even though he could not read or write. He began to tell us different stories about his life; from growing up as a little boy to the present. We sat there in awe with my father as he reminisced about his life. For a moment, it was as if we weren't sitting in a hospital room because of his illness. My father told my son that if anything should happen to him that he wanted Keith to have his car.

The main point my father wanted us to know was that God had been good to him. He shared with us the joy of working on a farm and being able to plant seeds and watch them grow over time. If something he planted didn't work out, it would teach him where he went wrong. The next year he would do something different. Over the years, he got better and better. Because he took such pride in his work, everyone around him knew whatever he planted was going to produce a harvest. He invested time into it. He watered, nurtured and put his love into it. He wanted his children to know if they do right and treated people right; then a harvest was going to come back to us. He shared that God had showed him favor from a little boy to his present age of 83. He said he realized he had a death day and he knew his was near. He was okay with that and knew that God did not make a mistake.

The doctor released my father with no major concerns other than his high blood pressure that he had most of his life.

The next day, in June 2015, I went back to his house and he couldn't even stand. I brought him back to the hospital and they said they were going to keep him. I left because I was confident he would be okay for the night. I called my father the next day to check on him. My father told me that he had a stroke that morning. I thank God he was at the hospital and not at home. He then had to go to rehab. From there things went downhill. I asked him why he was alone. I told him that I thought it was time for us to come together. I was so excited that God had chosen me to be there to care for my father during his final days.

When my father lived alone every neighbor began to tell him how blessed he was to have a daughter that was there for him. Every month when he received his check I would take care of his finances. There was never a concern about his finances. When he moved in with me no one could understand why I put my father's bedroom in the kitchen. God gave us the kind of apartment that allowed it to work for us. To us it really didn't matter. I was always at work. The thing that mattered most was that we were together and that he had someone to call. There was a time after my mother's death that he had to wonder who was going to care for him if he had gotten sick. Remember, my dad could not read or write. That was the main reason we had two different apartments. If something would have happened to me I didn't want him to have to try to relocate. I never wanted to burden him with the fact of wondering where he would live. Ever since I was a little girl I wanted to care for my dad.

Soon after we moved in together our relationship began to turn up-side down. At this time, I was working a full time and a part time job. Each morning before going to work I would get my dad up for breakfast and prepare his lunch and dinner. I also had to get him to his appointments. There was no one to visit or prepare a meal for him if I didn't. I really did not mind because he was my dad and I enjoyed caring for him.

Every day I would enter our apartment and have to listen to what the enemy, Satan, had been telling him all day. He began questioning me about what I was doing with his money and I would try to explain every penny. However, it did not matter. The enemy was trying to destroy our relationship. I never really learned how to budget money but I did learn how to pay my bills on time and learn how to save a little.

I had been delivered from drugs, but not from spending money. I always had to have more than enough of everything. I would keep a stack of Ensure. The refrigerator always had more than enough. It had gotten to the point where he was losing his appetite. I knew this was a sign that he was in trouble. I knew that death was not too far away. I would find myself crying in my bedroom because God was speaking to my heart, just as he had with my mother. He was telling me that the death angel was on his way.

There was chaos in the house once again. Every day he would com-plain about his money. He would tell me not to go shopping for him anymore; even when he was not able to shop for himself. I would want nothing but to see that my dad was okay after work. I also wanted to get a couple hours of sleep. It was like a mother with her child. I would hear my father calling for me because he was unable to move. I would have to dial 911 for medical assistance. The rescue team didn't have to think twice about the address because they were always there.

Satan was faithful in trying to destroy my relationship with my dad. There were times my dad would not say anything to me. I had to stand my ground. It was not always about money. I would say,

"Dad, you can't even walk. Why are you so concerned about money? You need to be praying."

I was watching him fade away. I had given him everything I possibly could and it wasn't enough. I could not let myself give him money just so he could give it away. I needed his money to be able to care for him. Satan had blinded him. I tried to explain to him that if I allowed someone to use him at that point than they would have been using me too. I had been used my entire life by men that I cared about. I had learned a long time ago how to treat my men like a King, while allowing them to neglect treating me like a Queen. I refused to allow the enemy to use me; even if it was my dad. I had to stand firm. I tried to explain my feelings to my dad over and over again. Every day people called to see what I had cooked or what I had spent his money on. It got to the point where I was about to lose my mind, but again, I refused to give in to the enemy. The enemy does not care how he gets to you or how he uses you. His job is to kill, steal, and destroy. I knew that if I would have given in, it would have started my obsession with men using me all over again. Not even my dad, who I love, could have taken me back to the emotional bondage I had been in for over twenty years.

I had experienced many hurts and pains from relationships. Men would always tell me they loved me, but they were never really there for me. I could never depend on them, but they could always depend on me. They knew if they needed me I was always going to be there. This was where this generational curse was going to be broken. At this end, I didn't care who it was. My father, my pastor, whoever... It was time to see if I was going to pass the test. The enemy knew that men were my weakness or should I say used to be my weakness? I finally got it. I could do badly all by myself. I passed the test. Was it easy? No. But you see; my father never realized that he was hurting me. Even though I was telling him,

"Dad, if I allow you to put me in a space I don't want to be in, then I am compromising my worth, dignity, sobriety, and my life. Most of all, if I allow you to do this to me it is the one thing that can destroy my relationship with God."

This is where the statement comes in: "*If you keep doing what you have always done, you will get what you always got.*" I know that God had delivered me from what I have always got. My father was not accustomed to women telling him no, especially his daughter. I loved and respected my father. I was his representative. I was there for him in every way that a daughter should have been. However, I was not willing to compromise what God had taught me and delivered me from. Men would never have their way with me again. This experience with my father made me feel as though I was still in a relationship with every man that I had been through.

I now realized that it was not so much about my dad wanting to give his money away. It was that it reminded me of all my brokenness experienced with men. Therefore, it was as if I was compromising. It was as if I was standing up for myself for not standing up to every man I had been with in the past. This time I was going to stand because my life depended on it. The cycle of all the times I would take care of men because I was in love with them but they were not in love with me had to be broken.

It hurt me so much for him to tell me that I took his driver's license from him. I had nothing to do with that. Through all the chaos I never left my dad's side. I can remember once when things got a little heated and I lost it. He could not understand why I didn't care about a friend that was in his life. I kept trying to explain to him that when someone really and truly cares about you then you will not have to ask for a thing. They will have your back automatically. They will just call when they see that you are as sick as you are. They will want to spend time with you. I watched my dad sit in the apartment every day without a visit.

I was always taking him back and forth to the hospital. When I got to the convalescent home he was sitting on the edge of the bed trying to do some physical therapy in front of the care aides. My dad told me,

"Brenda, they think I am lazy."

"Dad, you don't have to do another day of rehab."

I had to listen to people tell me that my dad wanted his own apartment. They couldn't see or didn't care that my dad was dying. My dad was unable to stay in the house alone. Here he is in this convalescent home dying from the end stage of Renal Disease. I said this not knowing that within two weeks my dad would no longer be with me. There I was, leaving work to go to the convalescent home to tell them that I was taking my dad out. This was God answering another prayer. I prayed for my dad not to pass away in the convalescent home. But, I was unable to take him home because he needed 24 hour care. It was as if no one could see that he was dying except me.

After being re-admitted back to the hospital, my dad was put on hospice. The Holy Spirit had already revealed this to me. I had worked in the medical field for years where God allowed me to comfort patients while they took their last breath. God allowed me to be there to give them their last rights; to make sure they knew who God was and that it was okay for them to die peacefully. What a great feeling for them to know that their maker was waiting patiently for them. God used me even in the midst of my drug addiction. I would always carry my little green bible everywhere I went. I would never go any place without it. My coworkers learned that when I walked into a patient's room with my little green bible out then it was not long before the death angel would come.

After the doctor explained that they had done all they could do without him agreeing to more dialysis, my dad finally realized it was too late for it. My dad was transported to another convalescent home. At this point I had lost so much time from work. I was trying to stay at work as much as possible. It was work one day and a call out the next. I thank God for my employer who was so understanding and there for me. My coworkers never complained if they had to work alone because I would sometimes have to call out within the hour of my shift beginning. They always wanted to know if there was anything they could do to help.

God used my son to be his grandfather's angel. My father had always been the only father that my son knew; therefore there was a special bond there. My son called me and told me that he had to try to get his grandfather on dialysis one more time. He wanted to remove him from the convalescent home and back to the hospital. The problem was that only I could do this as the person in charge. I called the doctor and told them to release my dad to my son. I called for transportation to take him back to the hospital.

There was one problem: we had to transport him to another hospital because the last hospital had "*Do not readmit*" on his file. My son stayed with my dad until I was able to get there. Here I was sleeping in another chair in another hospital. It wasn't a problem because it was where I wanted and needed to be.

I called my pastor and told him that my dad was dying. My pastor said he would be right there. He came on Sunday. He walked away from the congregation out of his love for me because he didn't want me to be by myself. He prayed for my dad and my dad thanked my pastor for coming. He told my pastor that God had been good to him and he lived a good life.

Even through all of this my dad still would not talk to me. He was still so angry with me. For days my dad lay in the hospital and would not say a word. I thought he couldn't talk because he was close to death. I know that his time on Earth was running out. One day Anthony and Latasha came to visit my dad and he began talking about how everyone thought he couldn't drive. He told them that he was upset because the doctor took his driver license a month earlier. I then realized where I had got my stubbornness from.

Three days before he died and the last time he talked, my dad opened his eyes and said,

"There's my baby,"

Just like he always used to say. That was the first and last time he talked to me in the hospital. He couldn't understand why I did not like his friend. But he knew that was the last time he was going to be able to say anything to me. In the end the enemy didn't win and God still got the glory.

He did not want me to have the joy of saying I took care of my dad because I had had so much joy from taking care of my mom and being there for her. Most of all I had joy because in the midst of my mess, God answered one of my biggest prayers. He was not going to allow me to have the same victory repeated. My dad's only brother, John D, and his daughter Allison never left his side. They were there every day until it was time for her to go to work.

My cousins Betty and Robert always saw the God in me from when I was a little girl. They were prayer warriors. My mom knew that and she would always call them for prayer. Once they heard about one of their favorite uncles being in trouble. They made the decision to make the trip. My father laughed and talked with them as if he was not sick. This turned out to be the last conversation my father would have.

Once again, I was able to spend the night with my dad. My grandson refused to leave his great grandfather's side. We knew we were in the final hours. I had the opportunity of praying and being by father's side as well. I watched my grandson Anthony pray for my dad. And then he began to sing the song *Gods going to break every chain,* by Tasha Cobbs.

ANTHONY'S PRAYER

"On the fifth day, God created the creatures of the waters and the birds of the sky, and then God made the creatures of the land. He created a man named Adam. God made the rainbow as a reminder of his promise to never again destroy so many living things."

This is what Anthony recited to me when the two of us were in our wildness. This blew my mind to know that I was not teaching him in vain and that God had revealed this to him at the right time. This was Anthony's way of letting me know that we were going to be okay. It was a reminder that God had brought us through trials before and He would do the same thing again.

It was exactly six months from the date of his stroke, to the day he was going to be with God. It was my wish that my dad did not die alone. How can I praise a God like this? Again, I had the pleasure of a loved one dying in my arms; truly a blessing for me. What the enemy meant for my bad, God used it for my good. The enemy meant to destroy our relationship, but he was not victorious.

CLOSING THE CHAPTER ON MICHAEL

I hid from Michael for over 20 years. One day I was driving down the highway going to work. This car kept blowing the horn at me and I was not going any faster so they might as well have went around me. I thought it was someone who wanted me to go faster. Finally, the car got close to me, because my mirror on the driver's side was broken off. I realized it was Michael and he was telling me to pull over on the highway. He said what drew attention to me was the broken mirror. He was a trucker and he noticed those things. Who would have thought after all those years I would run into him on the highway? I never thought I would be back having sex with him, but he began to come over and it was just as it was before. The fire was still lit because I had sex with Michael for many years before.

I was still trying to praise God in church and have sex with Michael. We were spending a lot of time together. Michael would come to church with me sometimes, but I would never allow him to sit with me at church. I didn't want anyone to know that we were together. He began to see that my shout was getting a little lighter and it was getting harder for me to praise God. We would talk about it and he told me that he would be the strong one and he wouldn't let me fall. He didn't want to hurt me. If that meant he had to walk away to let me be with God then he would walk away. He did just that. He stopped calling and stopped coming by. I still called him a couple of times. Even though we knew how to get in touch with each other we didn't for three years. I contacted him to tell him that my book was finally ready. We began to talk and I realized I was still in love with him. Michael asked me if I was still in love with him. He knew it was showing. When he asked me I couldn't say yes or no. I avoided the question all together. After a week I realized I was still in love with him. When we parted we were still in love. It was like my addiction was kicking in all over again.

Now it was easier for me to admit that I was still in love, but I was able to be free. After all these years I don't have to run anymore. I can face that I loved Michael and yet still not be with Michael. This is a chapter I can finally close. If I didn't think about Michael, it was as if he didn't exist. I ran for my life and my sobriety. I was afraid that my love for him would put me back with him. We always said and felt in our hearts that before we picked up the drugs together, we were awesome together. But, we can't take away the fact that we were drug addicts together. I'm just happy that I can close that chapter and know that I don't have to go back in time. I now know when God sends me a husband that I will be ready for him. I faced it and I'm ready to move on. I am a strong woman now. I loved Michael so much that it weakened me. If I didn't tell him how I felt than I would have never owned it. I just assumed that these men knew they hurt me, but I never told anyone until I told Michael.

My body wants to be with Michael. The lust is still there, but it's not right and I have to move on. I am royalty today. I have to stay praying and ask God to take away the lust because my flesh is weak. I can't allow my flesh to jeopardize what God has in store for me. I can't lie to myself. I have to pray and continue to trust God.

A COUPLE MONTHS LATER

God began to speak to me and I heard His voice again. A member's house had caught on fire and they had to leave their home. One Sunday the Holy Spirit told me to donate to them. A year later, when they moved back into their home, they invited me over for dinner. I thought a lot of people were going to be there, but when I got there it was my pastor's family and I. They had so much food and they treated me like a queen. I was so happy because no one ever did anything for me. It was always me giving. I sat at home that night and meditated to God. He spoke back to me and told me it was time for me to tell my story. He told me to call my pastor right now. I called and told him and he told me to call his wife. She fully supported and told me to pick my date. The church would host my book release. I began to write this book and I lost my money in the process. I didn't receive a book because the publisher took my money. When the date came the Holy Spirit told me I was the book and I didn't need the book. People came from everywhere and the anointing was there. People lifted their hands and cried before God. God was showing me that He could see the lilies of the field. He allowed so many people to come to my home that day to feed them. I then brought them to my church and fed them my word. Once upon a time I was worried about feeding myself, but at this time I fed so many other people. I took it as a learning experience. God told me that the thirty-five page book was not the book I wanted. It took that publisher to motivate me. Out of everything bad there is good in it. Here we are three years later and the real book is here.

KEEP GOD FIRST

I thank God for grace and mercy. It was His grace and mercy that saved me. God placed angels all around me to guide me in the right direction. If it had not been for His grace, I know without a doubt there were only three places for me to go: institution, jail, or death. God didn't see any of those fit for me. God took my mess and turned it into my testimony. He kept me here to tell my story. The day God made a covenant with me when my mom died was my turning point. To this day God has not failed me. He honored every promise He gave to me. He has restored everything the locust worm took from me.

I realized that I trusted Him with everything but my heart. I have asked God to take me off drugs and to strengthen my relationship with Him. I have asked God to restore my relationship with my son and allow me to be a part of my grandchildren's life. I asked Him to restore material things, but I have never asked God to restore my broken heart because I never knew it was broken.

God has allowed people, places, and things to get me through my past and present season. I thank the Lord for every tear I have shed. It helped mold me into the person I am today. I love me today and I could not always say that. I could never find the words to express my love to God. I love to show God through my walk, shout, praise, and my tears. Every praise that I have is to my God. This is not just a Sunday thing. An apostle once told me that I have grown. I asked what she meant. She said,

"Look at your hands. You don't have burns all over your hands anymore."

I had to learn to love myself again. I learned at an early age how to make a man my king, but I never took the time to allow them to make me their queen; to allow them to take care of me. I never realized I was the one giving everything. I never learned how I was to be treated. I never noticed that they had stopped loving me and the relationship was not 50/50 any-more, except for the lust. I allowed lust to control my life.

I had to admit that I have been in love with every man that I have been with. Even though the relationship was over, I was never able to tell them how much they hurt me. I was never able to put closure to anything. I was not able to let go. I gave my power away. I never lost money in the relationship; I lost myself, which was more powerful than money. This is for every man that I have allowed to abuse me physically, mentally, verbally, and emotionally. I just got my deliverance through writing about Michael in this book. All glory to God!

I wiped Jesus' feet with my tears. I had to repent for every woman's husband that I have slept with; everything that I have ever stolen, and every lie I have told.

I thank God I am a mother to my son, because I wasn't always a mother to him. I thank God for my grandchildren. I thank God for being able to repent. I thank God for loving and caring parents that never stopped loving and caring for me. I am dedicating this book to them.

When it looked like I had no place to stay God stepped in right on time and gave me the very best. In my very first treatment about thirty years ago, when I claimed I wanted a sports car, God gave me my dream car. God will exceed above all you can ask for. Through that car, no matter where I go, I always get a compliment on it. It is a door I can open to tell them how great our God is and give Him glory. I always had a faith that God would never leave me or forsake me. I held on to that for the good and the bad times. I thank God for the praise and confidence to allow me to get in the center aisle and not care what people think. They didn't know my story but if they did perhaps they would be right there with me. My prayers and faith have allowed me to move mountains. Through Him I was delivered from smoking two packs of cigarettes a day. After everything I have been through I have never picked up a cigarette again. I have never picked up a drug or alcohol since then and I know that was God who delivered me. God has turned my tears into joy.

It is my desire to go deeper in His word to allow this book to reach the broken hearted, touch the addicts, touch the abused, and to touch people who want to know more about God. I desire to open doors and talk about God; how He will take us from the bottom to the top. No matter what you are going through God will help you through it. I want to let you know that whatever you've been through God is still able to have you hold your head up and walk in your authority. He is just waiting on us to ask Him what we want.

Yes, sometimes we get hurt in the church, but we have to remember why we are there. Yes, we might be sensitive, but we can't be so quick to walk away. We have to know our worth. God allowed me to walk on water all through my praise and faith. Faith is a big part of who I am today. Without faith and knowing there was a God who would and could deliver me from crack cocaine; I wouldn't have made it. God came and took away all of my shame, guilt, and lust. Before God could deliver me from the drugs, he had to deliver me from lust.

I thank God that I can recognize abuse. I don't have to let anyone strip me like a banana. Before we know it, little by little, we become so broken. I thank God that out of everything I have been through, I am still standing. I am still in my right mind and I still have peace, joy, and a relationship with God. Now I can take all that energy and go deeper in His word.

I know this was my calling and my purpose. I was just too fearful to walk in it before. I believe in my heart that this is what this book is for. God has equipped me with this book that will allow me to walk through different doors to reach people like myself wherever He sees fit to send me. Everyone is not going to see the value and the worth that God places over your life. Sometimes God will have you to step out and use you in another way. I was looking for God to use me in the church for drugs and alcohol. However, that's not the way God chose to use me. He is using me in the street; just where my mess was. God uses me to minister to the broken hearted so He can heal them. God took me from the base house to the kingdom. He took me from being called base head to being called Ms. Brenda.

I have watched strong people walk in their destiny because they were not afraid to allow God to use them. I am asking God to remove the fear away from me and others. It is God that has qualified me to relate to sick and suffering addicts who don't realize God is able. For that reason, God has allowed me to share stories of where my addiction has taken me.

Currently I have two jobs, my own place, a nice car, people who care about me, and most importantly a strong relationship with God. I thank God for all the people He allowed to touch my life. Thank you to all the people that prayed for me and all the people that believed in me. I could never thank God enough.

Signed, Sealed and Delivered Brenda Martin: From Broken to Blessed!

About the Author

Brenda Tiller Martin is a mother, grandmother, friend, and mentor. She was born and raised in Alabama and moved to Hartford, Connecticut at nine years old. Brenda was pregnant and married at a young age. Brenda entered into a world of drugs and alcohol and found herself in multiple abusive relationships. Brenda mistook lust for love. She was headed down a one-way street and was addicted to crack cocaine for 19 years. God reached down to her at her lowest point and touched her. God told her chasing Him was better than chasing lust. Through many years of brokenness, disappointment, depression, and not wanting to live any longer, Brenda was able to overcome all of this and graduated college with an associate's degree as a drug and alcohol counselor. She has touched many lives as a mental health worker. God has allowed her to hold her head up through it all and share her story. She believes that through her words you will find inspiration and hope. No matter how low you are, if you just have faith, you too will be set free and made whole. Brenda is enjoying her journey as an author and is currently working on her next book.

Contact Brenda at BrendaTillerMartin@gmail.com

45064357R00096

Made in the USA
Middletown, DE
23 June 2017